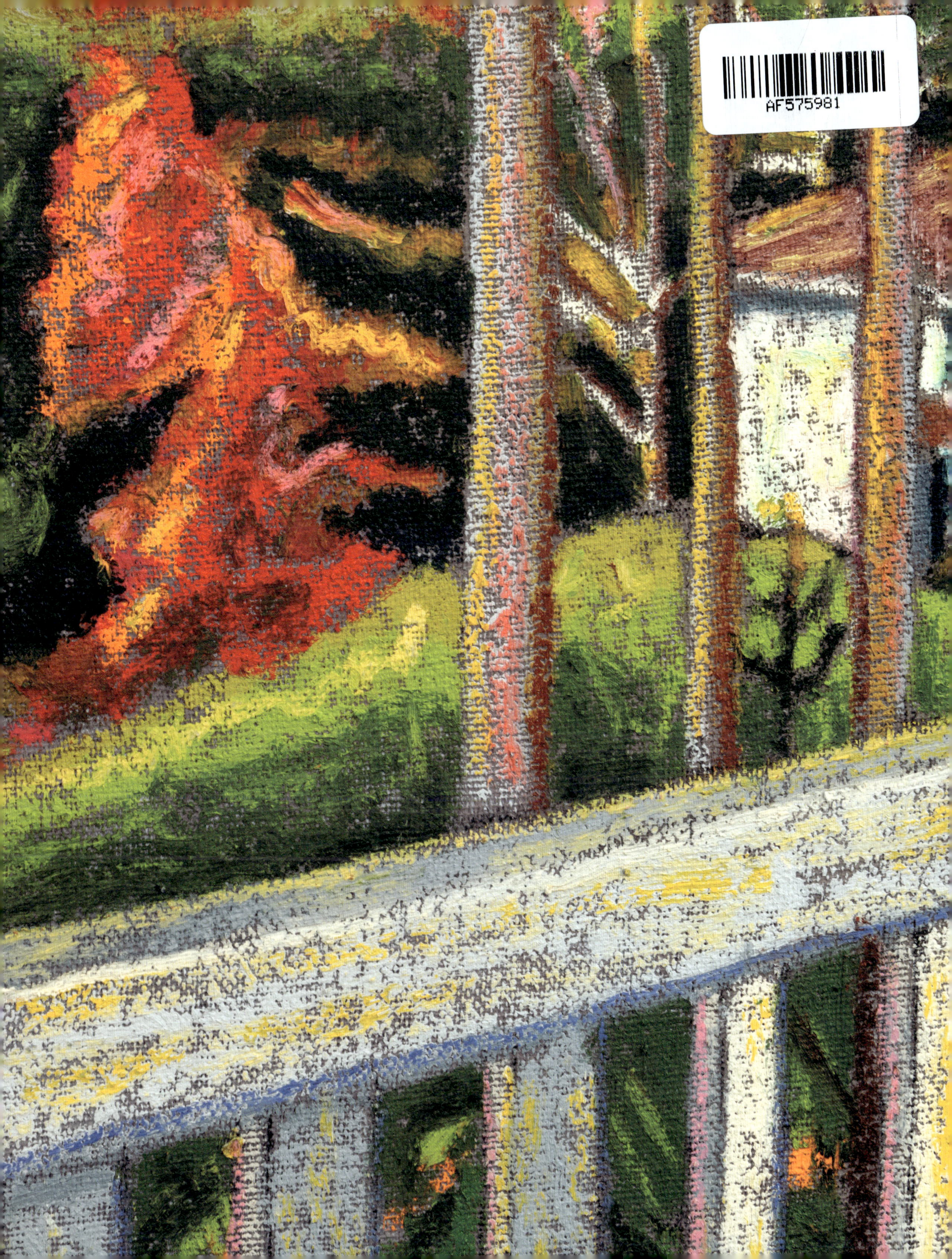

Published in the United States by Derek Eller Gallery and Harper's

Designed by Tod Lippy

www.derekeller.com / www.harpersgallery.com

ISBN: 978-0-9779002-9-9

First Edition

Printed and bound in Canada

JJ MANFORD

DEREK ELLER GALLERY / HARPER'S

2024

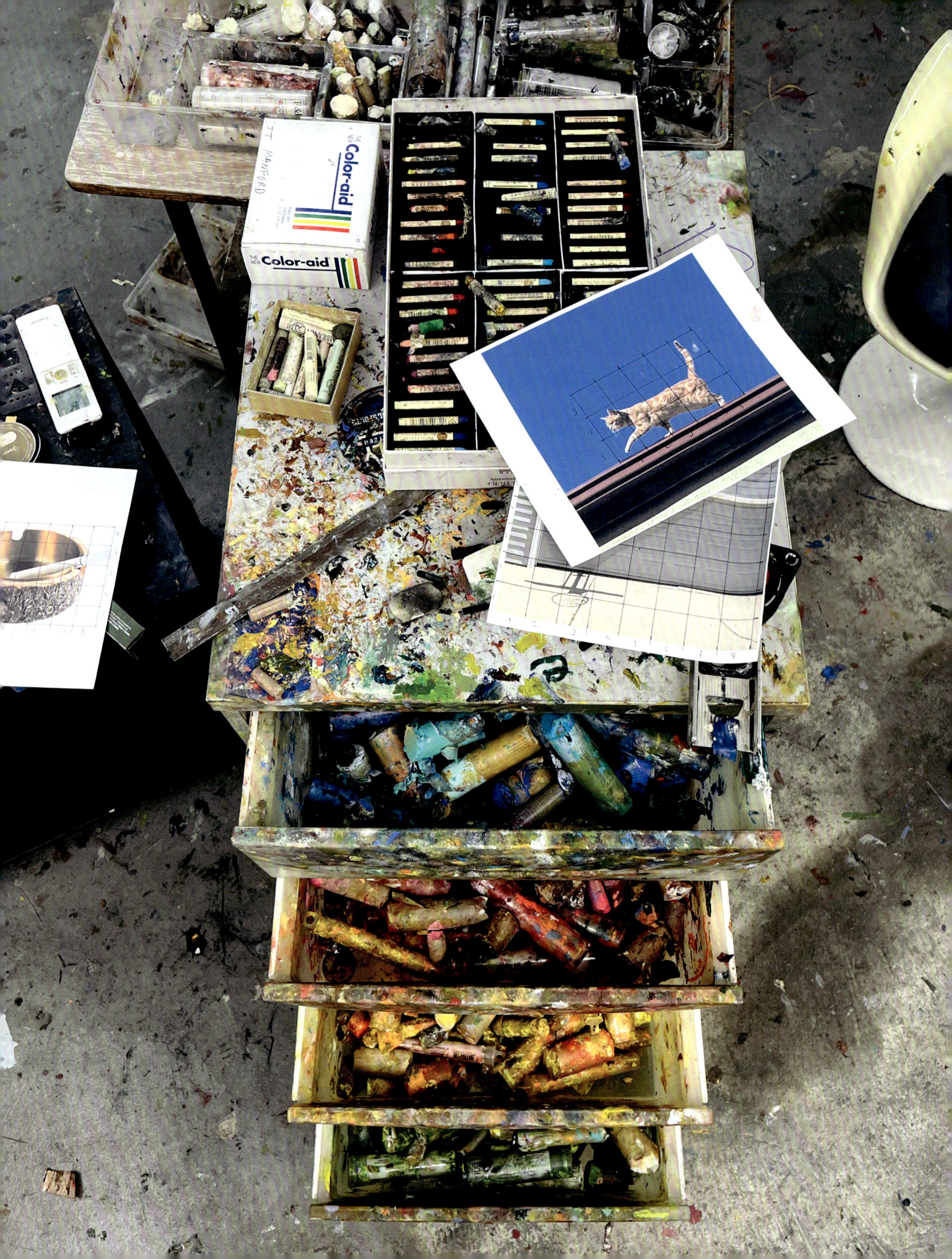
THE NEW Color-aid
THE NEW Color-aid

JJ Manford: In Living Color

By Gilles Heno-Coe

"I enjoy taking a banal image and sort of infusing it with life."

JJ Manford's enigmatic interior tableaux vibrate with animate intensity despite the characteristic absence of life, save for an occasional potted plant or loafing tabby cat. With a sure yet searching hand, Manford lays down thousands of vibrant marks in oil stick and oil pastel onto large stretches of burlap or linen, transforming these otherwise subtly surreal domestic scenes into scintillating fields of luxurious texture and lively color. Manford's paintings are apt embodiments of the term *still life*, unless you take into account the gradual incorporation of landscape into his more recent work.

Signs of life are exactly that. Life is inferred instead of depicted, connoted by Manford's finely tuned juxtapositions of interiors and domestic objects, which serve as surrogates for absent inhabitants. Usually appearing as fashionably clad suburban dwellings decorated with an eclectic grouping of furnishings, Manford's paintings sometimes possess the air of a Christie's catalogue, at other times one for domestic furnishings. This is *Martha Stewart Living* meets David Lynch, but not as foreboding. His paintings are placid, but with the occasional air of anxiety or nostalgia (usually both). High and low happily, stylishly, commingle.

"The image is just a jumping-off point for invention that happens while I'm painting."

Despite the obvious significance of his chosen objects and interiors, it would be a mistake to neglect Manford's laborious technical process, given the fundamentally affective role it plays for artist and viewer. His systematic method of repetitive and layered mark-making accommodates both plan and improvisation, besides being simply the most economical means of quickly, but precisely, covering an area with color. The overall effect lies somewhere between the vibrant expressivity of Pierre Bonnard and the Post-minimal fastidiousness of Chuck Close.

He begins with a stretched bolt of linen or, alternatively, burlap mounted to to linen, the latter of which has a loose and irregular weave ideal for catching large gobs of oil stick, especially suitable for the largest scale works. Manford appears to work most comfortably at a large scale, although his smaller works present an interesting challenge in terms of mark size and image resolution.

The stretched fabric is gessoed with grey, a fundamental color for Manford. He takes fullest advantage of this neutral ground, painting it first with a layer of dilute Flashe, a vinyl matte medium, in an array of colored gradients loosely reminiscent of an Ellsworth Kelly spectrum. Over this, a regular grid is drawn as an armature for the eventual composition, which will be outlined in charcoal, a process demanding exacting draftsmanship. While Manford occasionally alters compositions after entering the final phases of oil coloration, it is considerably more difficult by then and requires great technical skill to work against such an indelible medium. In spite of this, Manford is becoming more comfortable with compositional improvisation and it is allowing him greater flexibility with his final choice of imagery.

A resulting effect of successive paint layering is an appealing tension between the depicted light source (oil overpainting) and the actual light source (the luminous effects of the underpainting). Another result is a tension between depicted and actual depth—the paintings are all remarkably flat, optically speaking—yet close up, they reveal a texture created through the successive layering of individual marks, which often take weeks to dry. The visual effect is also akin to that of digital pixelation, made palpably manifest. Manford's colors are not the colors of real life, but they are indeed vital, living colors.

The images themselves are usually, but not always, chosen from stock photographs gathered from online sources and saved in bulk on his iPhone. Some have explicitly personal significance, while others are chosen for more formal reasons. They are also printed out on standard sheets of printer paper—battered and torn from repeated referencing—which rise in teeming reams on tables in his studio among large trays of oil pastels and used bits of charcoal.

Manford cites a casual indebtedness to art and architectural history, but not to any sort of formal school or ideology. His practice is pragmatic and intuitive, not dogmatic or prescriptive. Yet artworks by noted artists past and present are liberally depicted in his scenes, revealing something of his own taste as well. Works by Picasso and Miró appear in Manford's rooms, as do those of Mose Tolliver, William Hawkins, or Gee's Bend quilters.

Manford likens his work to collage and, in passing, praises the pioneering assemblage artist and filmmaker Joseph Cornell, whose gem-like box constructions and collages resonate with a frequency similar to that of Manford's paintings. As Manford explains, "The interior is an armature for combining disparate imagery to create some sort of chemistry between objects, which is a collage, in a way." His choice of imagery is deliberate, but subtle, with rhymes, redundancies, counterpoints, a whole drama unfolding metaphorically and visually between and among interiors and their furnishings, from Kachina dolls and Noguchi lanterns to Picasso posters and Moroccan rugs.

Sometimes architectural history is explicitly invoked, less as a painted object than as overt subject, as one might glean from Manford's repeated invocation of Frank Lloyd Wright and Le Corbusier. The depicted scenes are also usually quite shallow, extending to just one or two rooms, sometimes with a glimpse of the outdoors as seen through a door or window. He makes fastidious use of linear perspective, an effect that sometimes causes the image to seem to pop out or vibrate against an otherwise flat surface. Manford may choose backdrops and objects more banal or commercial, reminiscent of stock photos from glossy 1980s design and lifestyle magazines or Home Depot deck-furniture spreads.

In all these paintings, however, a sense of absence lingers. Though life may be explicitly absent, Manford's paintings are hardly deadened. The objects and walls and picture frames and couch cushions are infused with it, embodied foremost by his highly expressionistic color combinations. The objects and interiors also serve as substitutes for the missing occupants, inferred to be either Manford, or, through projection, ourselves. Chosen in one sense for their formal significance within the composition, objects nevertheless become symbolically resonant, representing aspects of a missing persona's personality or lifestyle. What kind of person might own a Keith Haring rug or a Siamese cat? Who hangs the poster of an artwork versus the thing itself?

Manford confirms that recent works, in particular, have a person-

OPPOSITE: JJ Manford's Brooklyn studio, November 2023. Photograph by JJ Manford.

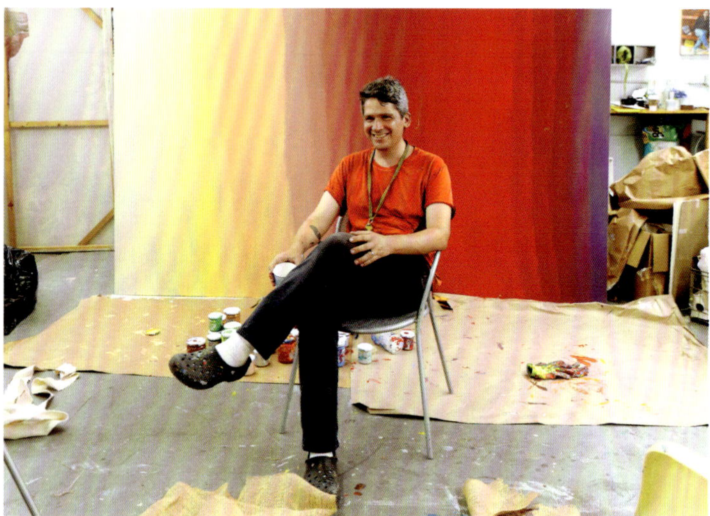

JJ Manford in his Brooklyn studio, November 2023. Photograph by Olya Frank.

ally nostalgic bent, reflecting his adolescence in 1980s and 1990s New England. Objects like Sonic the Hedgehog toys, Bart Simpson figurines, or *Where the Wild Things Are* posters evoke this particular ambience. Speaking about a recent painting of a vintage car interior, Manford recalled the exact smell of the leather seats, decades later. Another painting triggers a poignant memory from childhood about the pain and awkwardness of growing up.

These paintings are all about life, as it turns out.The artist's as well as ours. We bring to his work many of our own associations and memories, especially those of us who grew up in the same generation as he did. The absence of the human figure—in spaces that are depicted almost life-size—makes the viewer sensitive of their own embodied presence. As if to underscore this fact, Manford has recently made room-size rugs and ottomans based on those depicted in several of his paintings. The designs are his, but they originated in the paintings themselves, highlighting a constant give-and-take between art and life that occurs in his work.

Within the last year, landscape has become more prominent in Manford's paintings, in some cases displacing the interior as the main compositional element. While parts of the landscape are sourced from stock photographs as well, they allow Manford a much greater range of expressive potential, both in composition and choice of palette. Like his rugs and ottomans, the landscape gives him freer reign. Yet his landscapes are always anchored by an architectural element: a door frame, a wooden deck, a backyard fence. This is not landscape experienced raw, but rather mediated by domesticity. This particular compositional strategy of balancing the interior and outdoor spaces, oddly enough, throws into relief just how domesticated the landscape already is.

Manford's work broadly inhabits a similarly liminal space, somewhere between invention and appropriation, painting and drawing, experimentation and design, inside and outside. It is carefully tuned, like his color combinations. Musical analogies are appropriate in this instance, as he himself has acknowledged. These are not paintings about life, per se, but they demonstrate that longing of wanting to give life to something. But that has long been the domain of artists—to bring inanimate matter to life. Manford succeeds in that regard, if only to remind us that sometimes even the most banal parts of life can still be both wonderful and strange.

All quotes from JJ Manford are taken from interviews or correspondence with the author in November 2023.

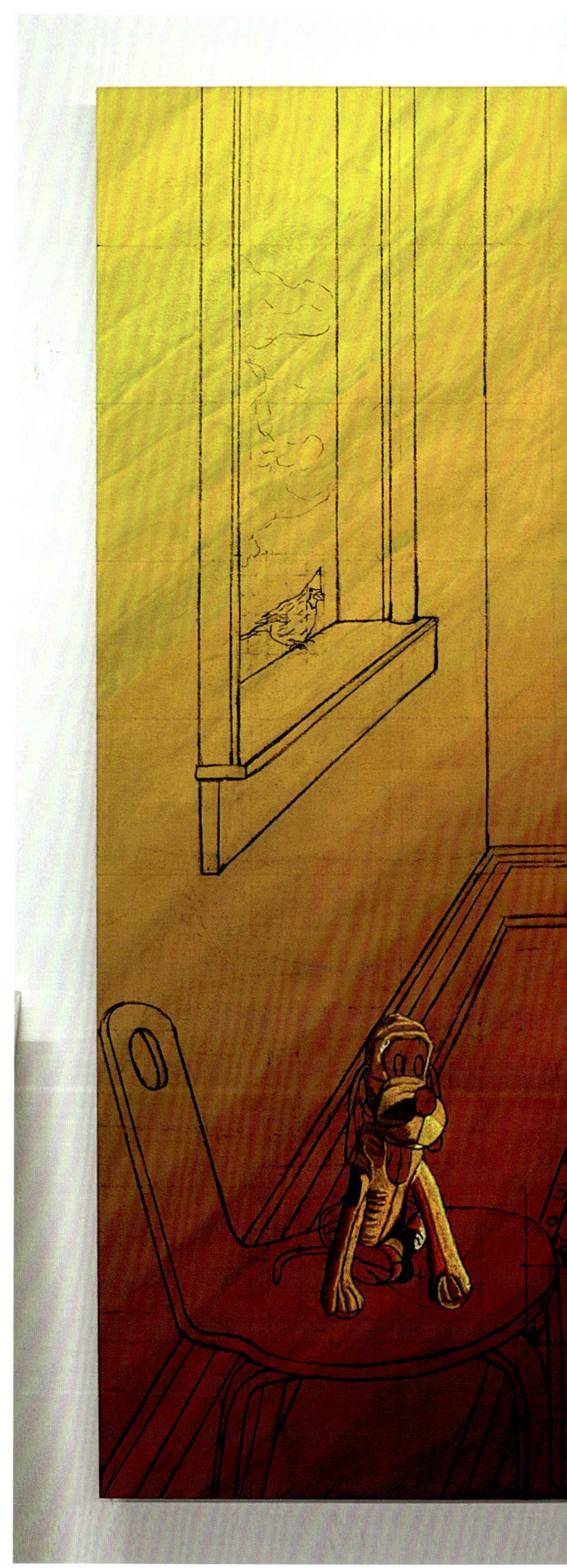

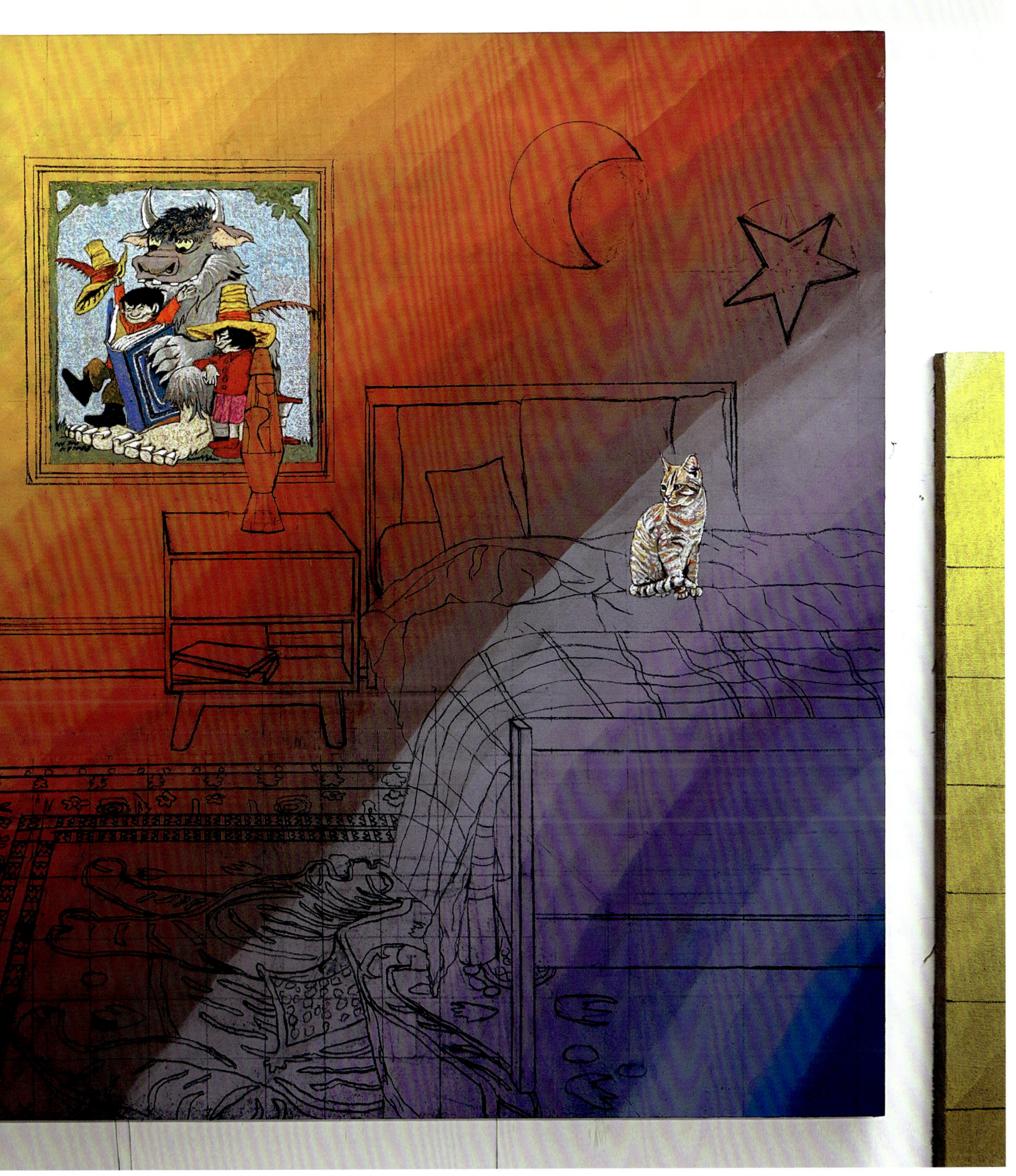

Unfinished version of *Childhood Bedroom with Lava Lamp, Pluto, and Wild Things Poster* in Manford's Brooklyn studio, August 2023. Photograph by Tod Lippy.

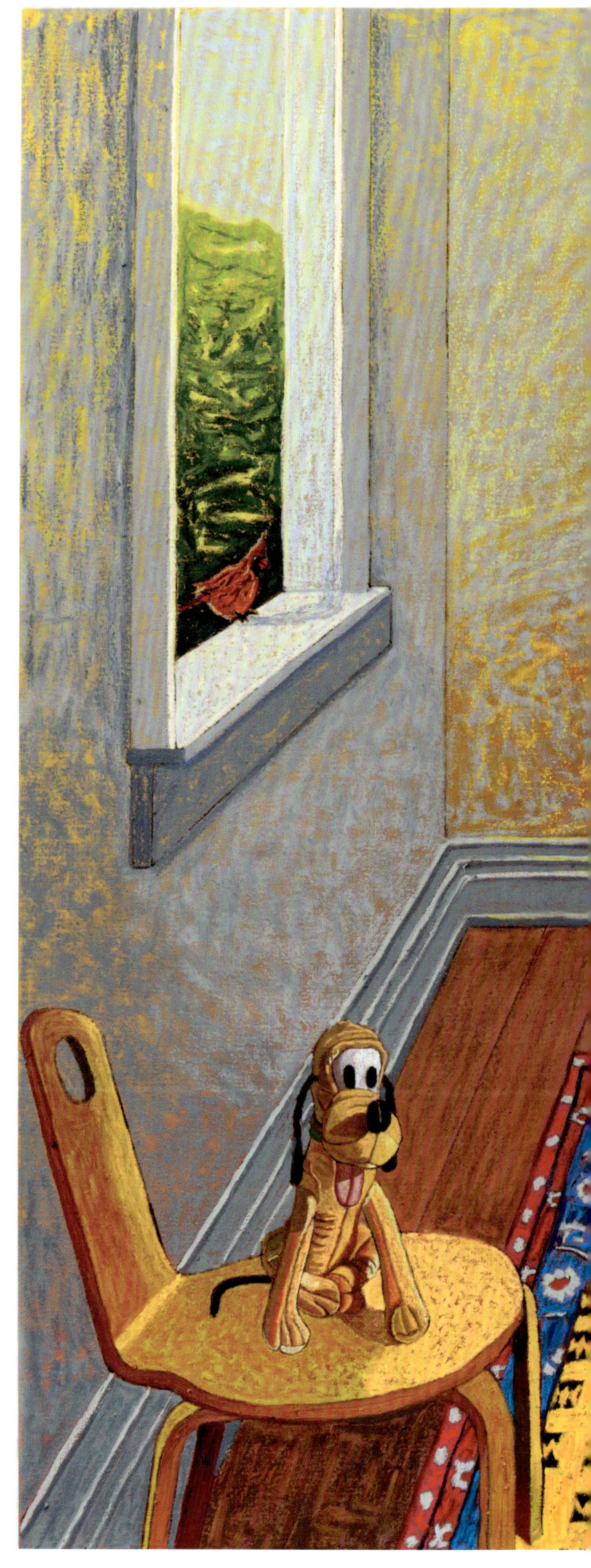

Childhood Bedroom w

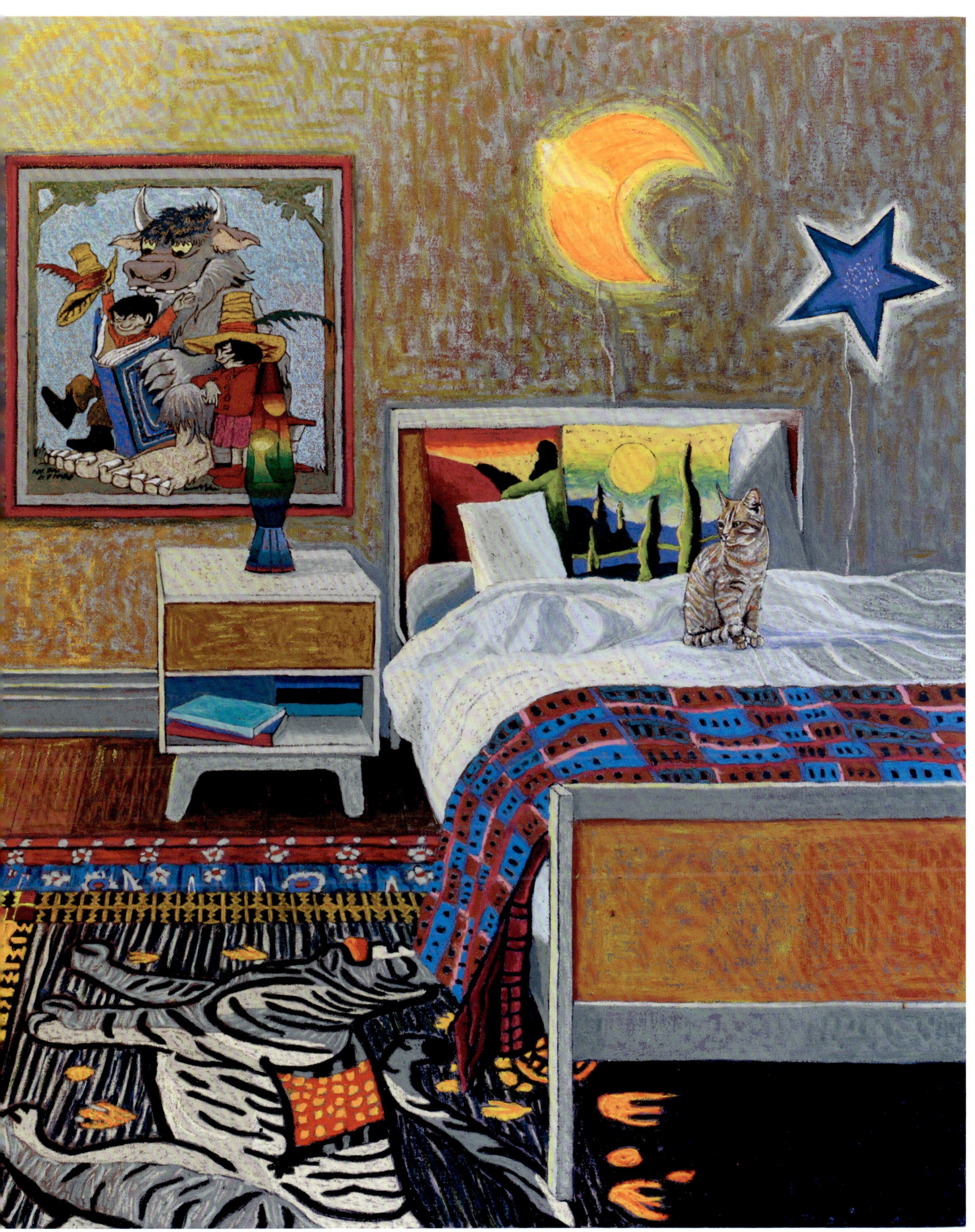

'a Lamp, Pluto, and Wild Things Poster, 2023, oil stick, oil pastel, and Flashe on burlap over canvas, 90 x 112 inches

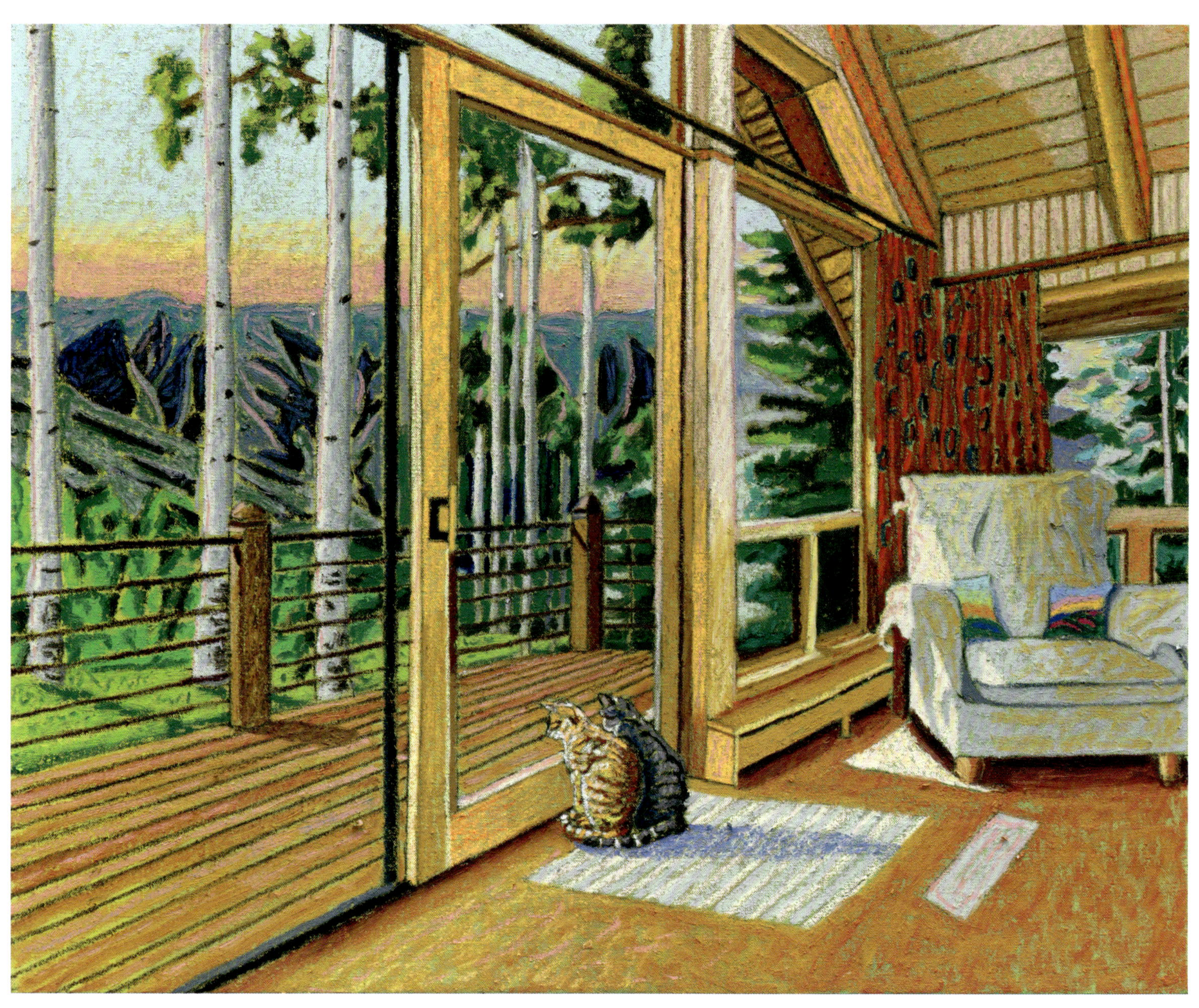

Aspen Summer (Love Cats), 2023, oil stick, oil pastel, and Flashe on linen, 36 x 45 inches

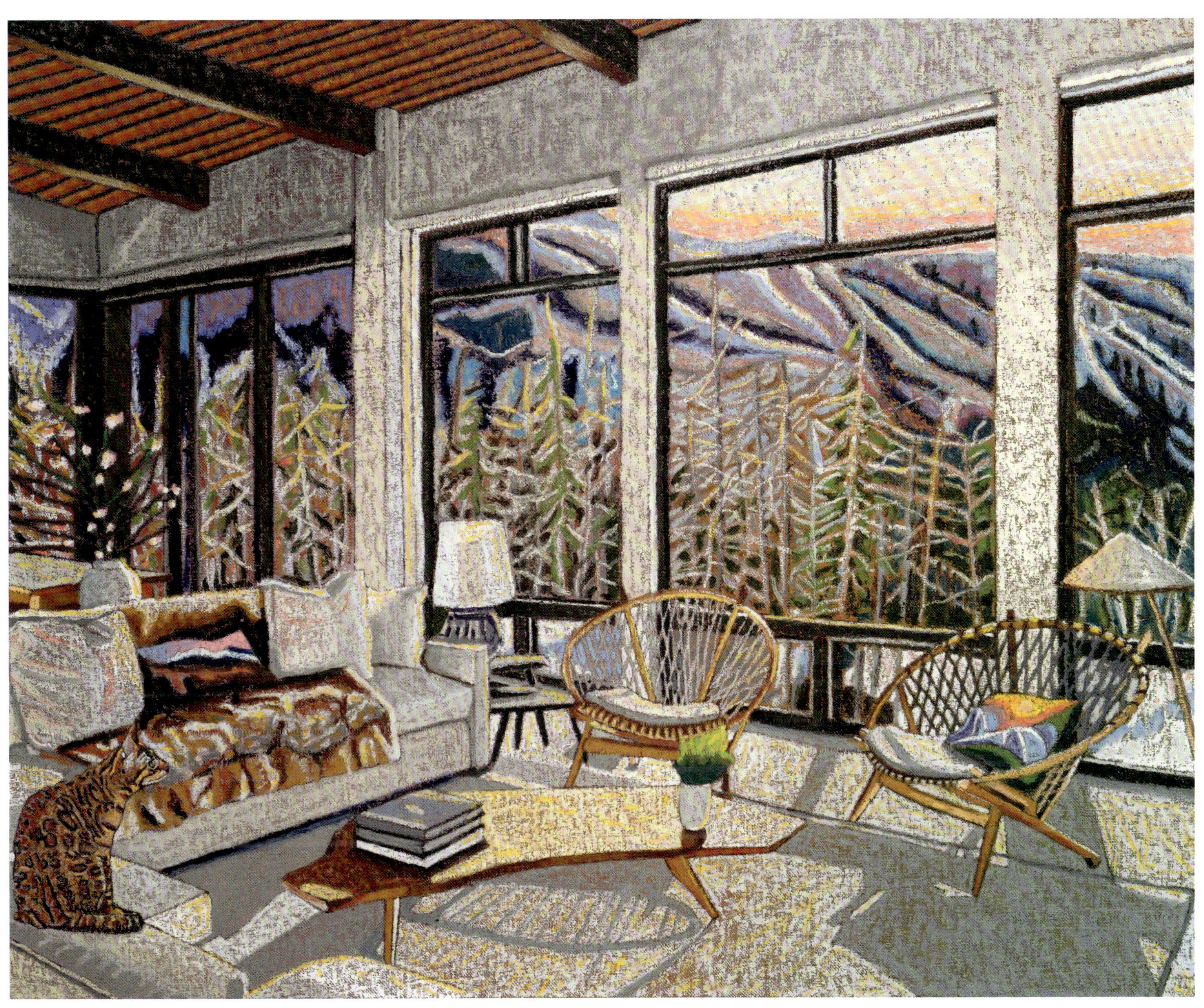

Alpineglow Ski Lodge Painting, 2023, oil stick, oil pastel, and Flashe on burlap over canvas, 68 x 85 inches

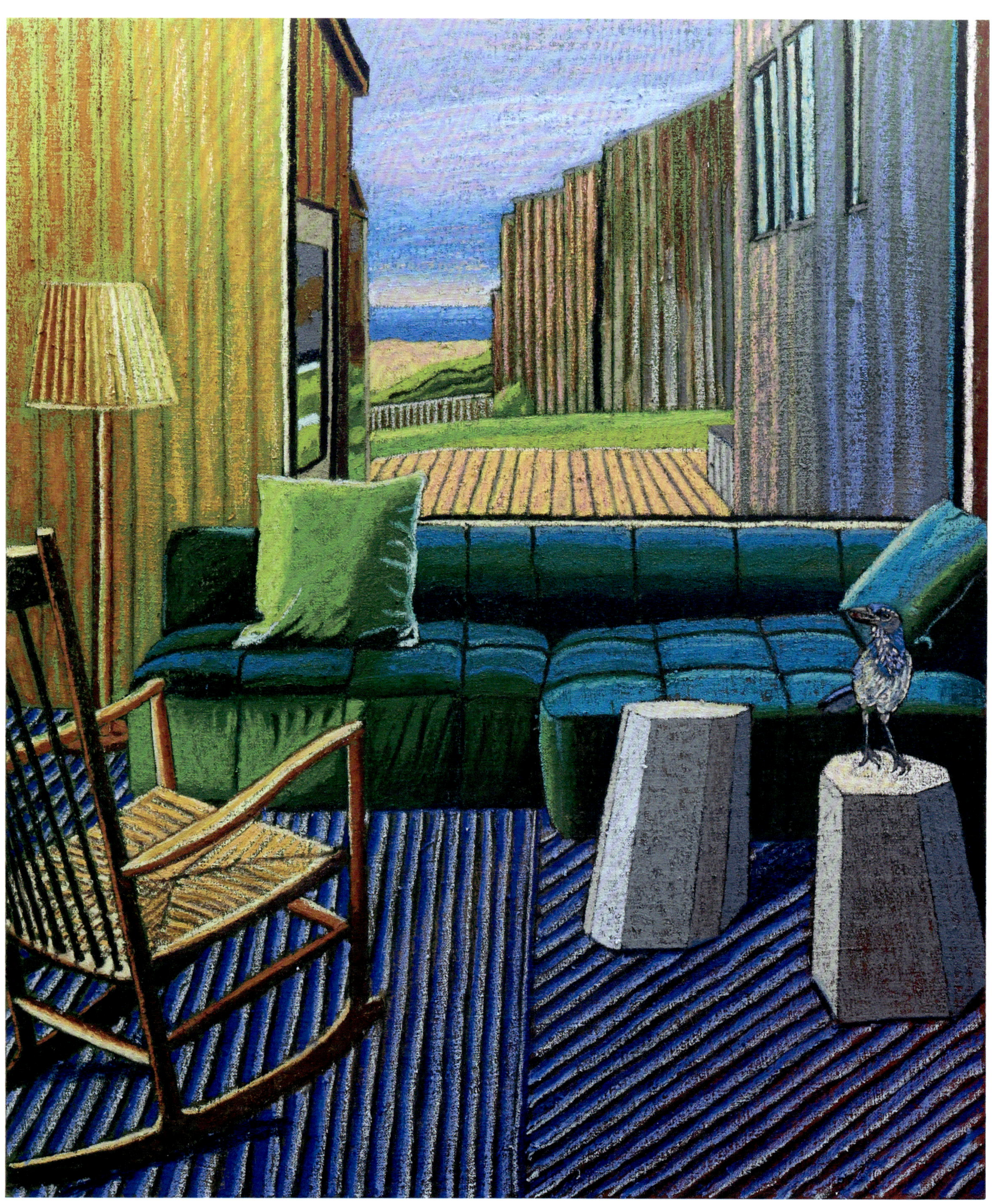

Sunset at Sea Ranch with California Scrub Jay, 2022, oil stick, oil pastel, and Flashe on burlap over canvas, 84 x 72 inches

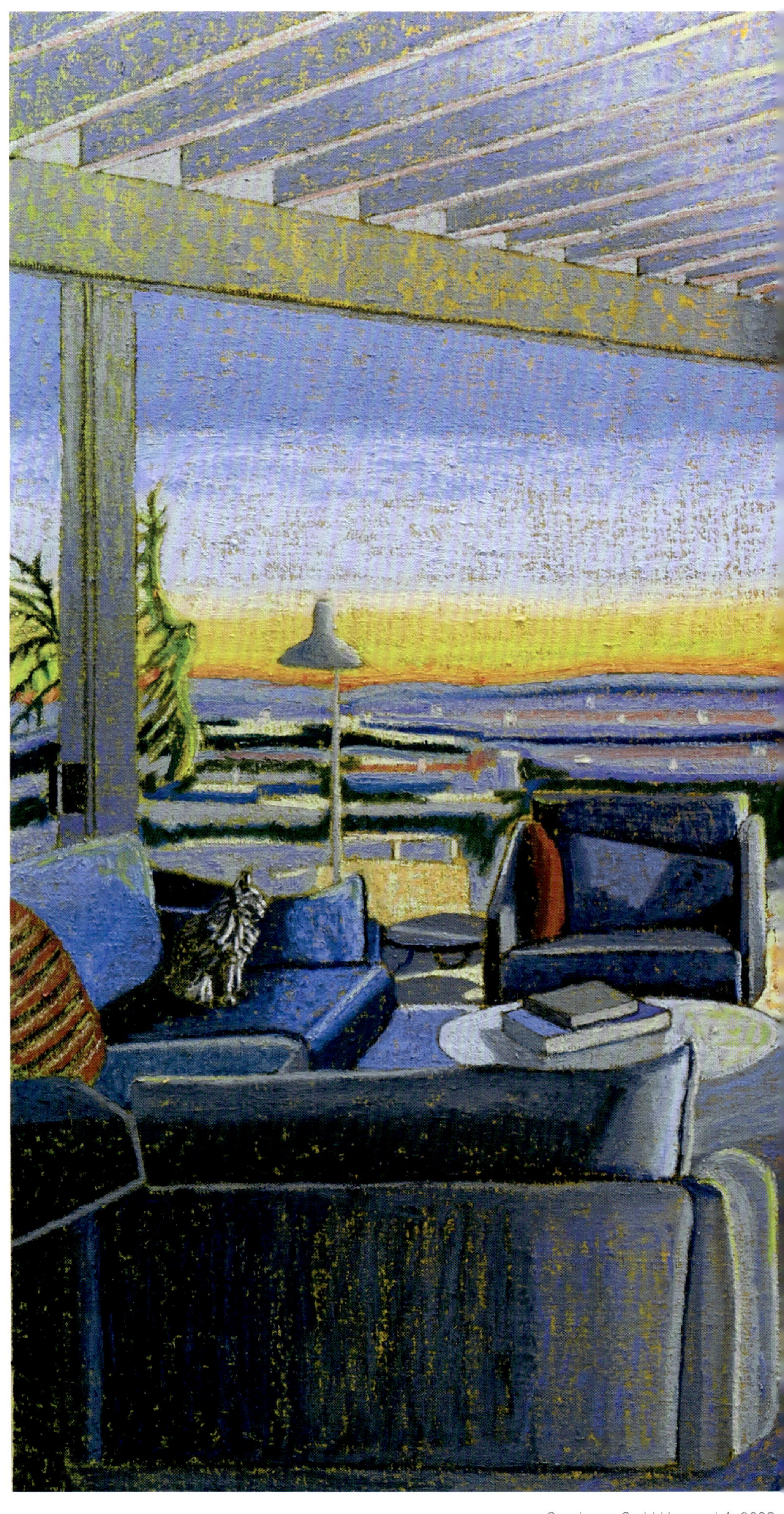

Sunrise at Stahl House, LA, 2023,

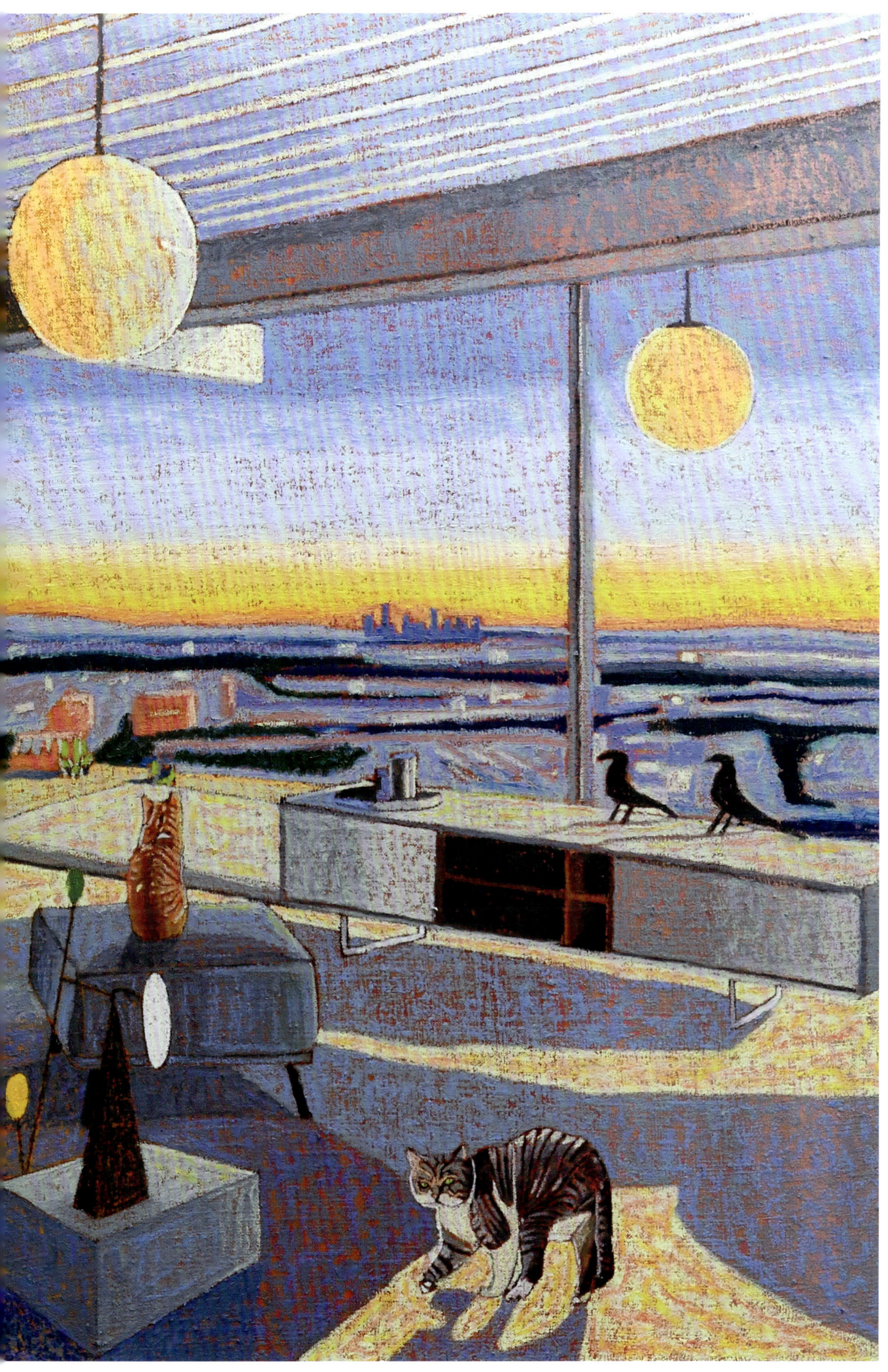

×, oil pastel, and Flashe on burlap over canvas, 88 x 110 inches

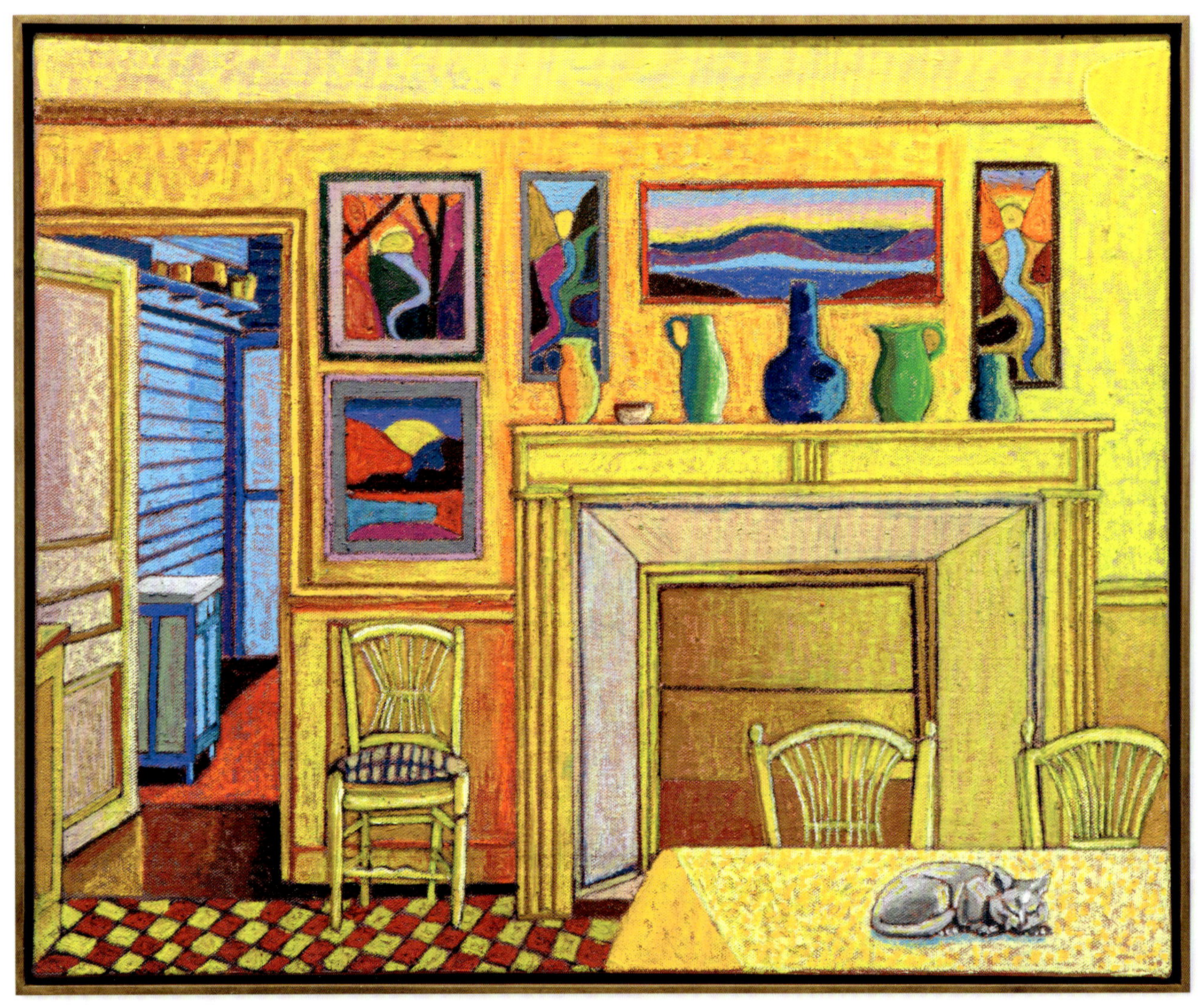

Monet's Porcelain Cat, 2023, oil stick, oil pastel, and Flashe on linen, 24 x 30 inches

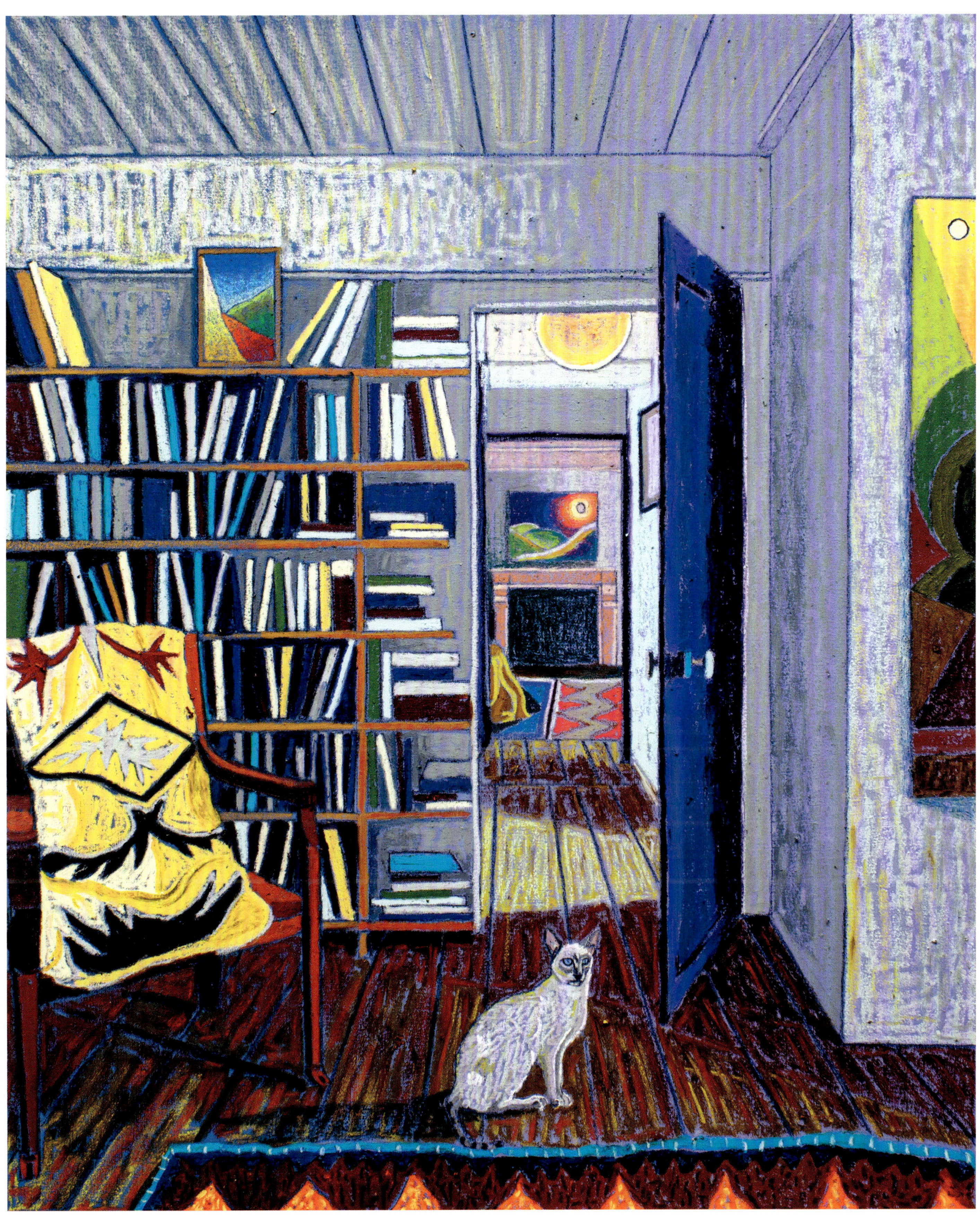

Library with Siamese Cat, 2021, oil stick, oil pastel, and Flashe on linen, 60 x 50 inches

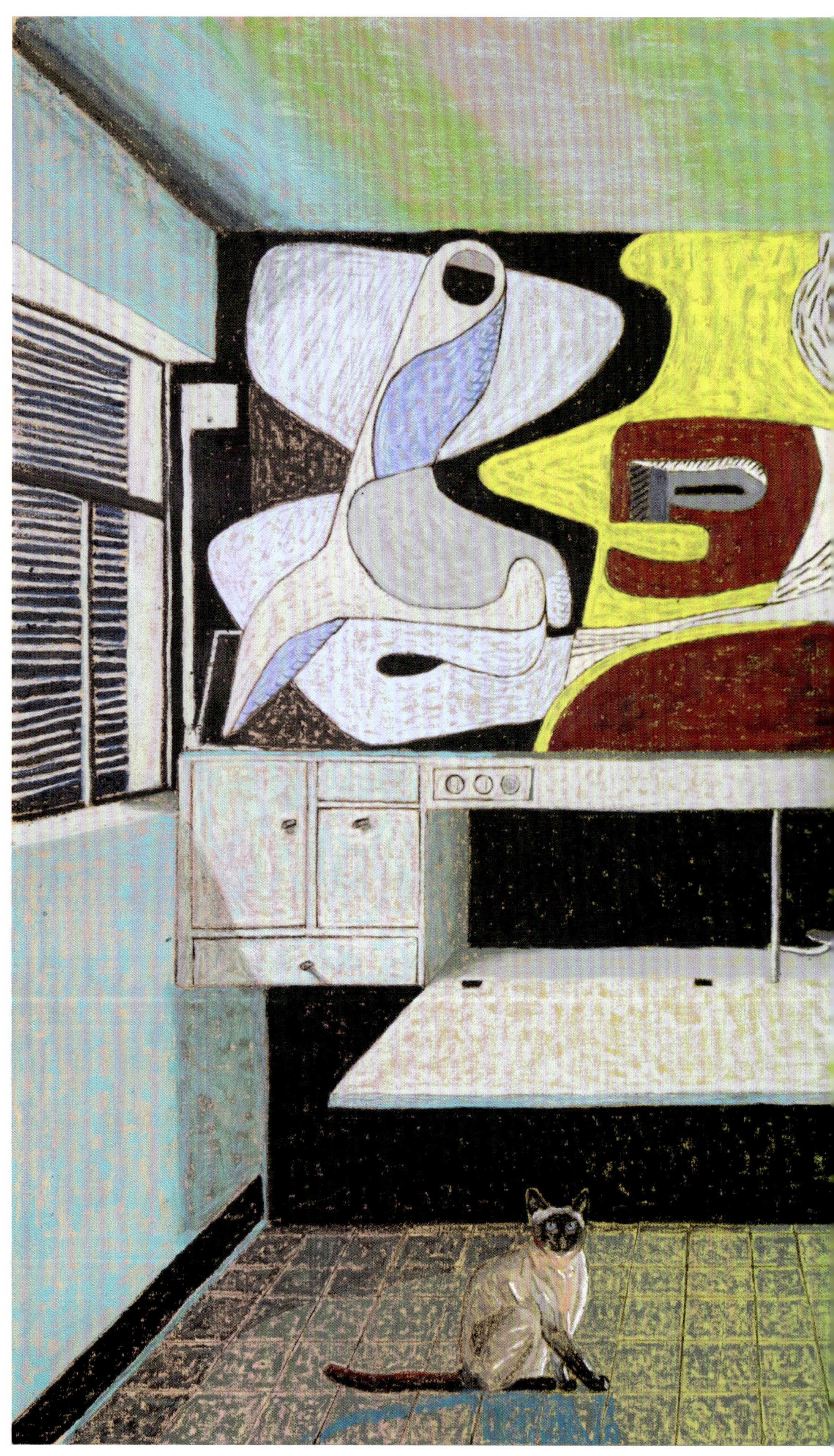

E-1027 Interior with Siamese Cats, 2022, oil s

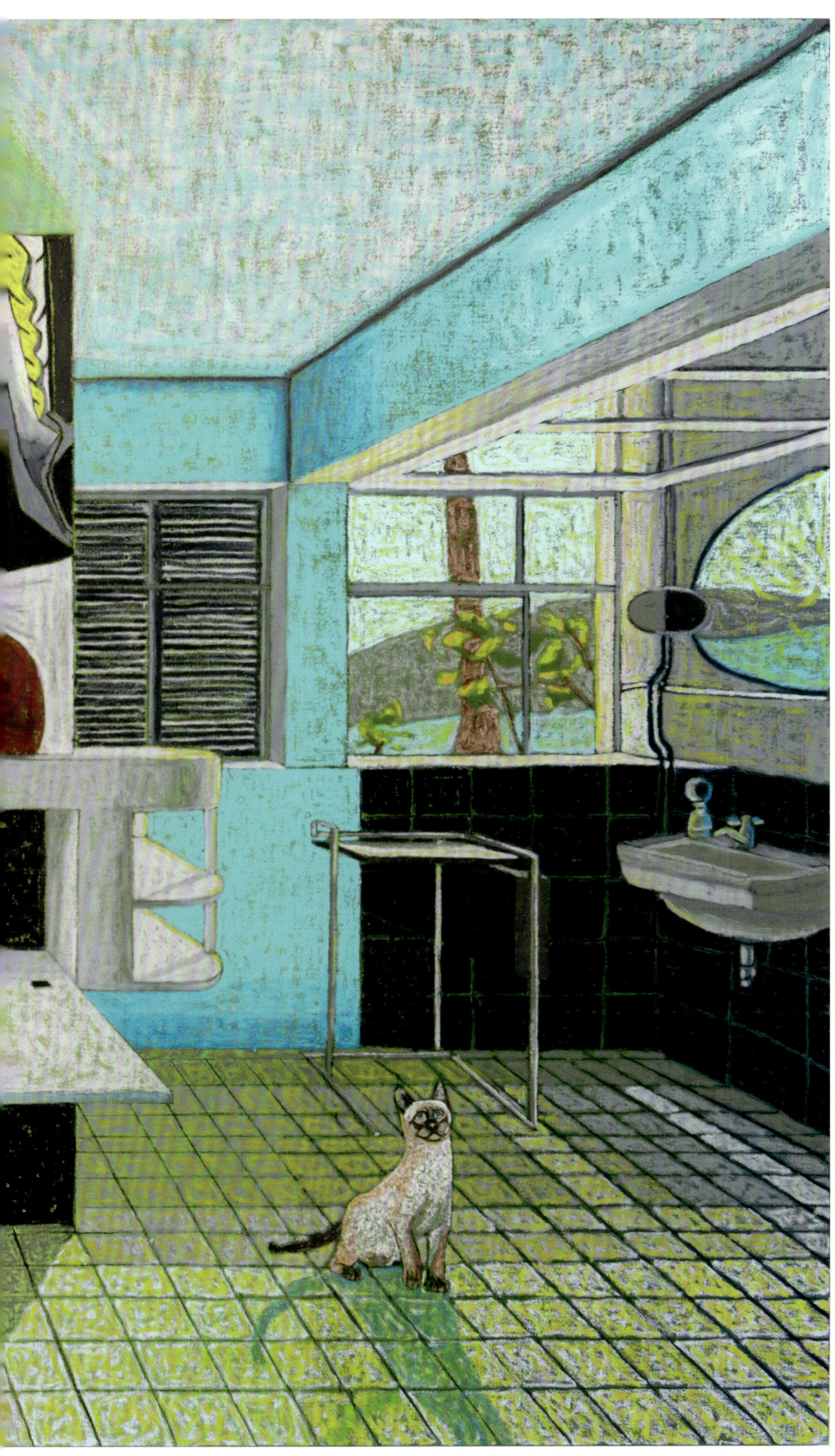

pastel, and Flashe on linen, 90 x 112 inches

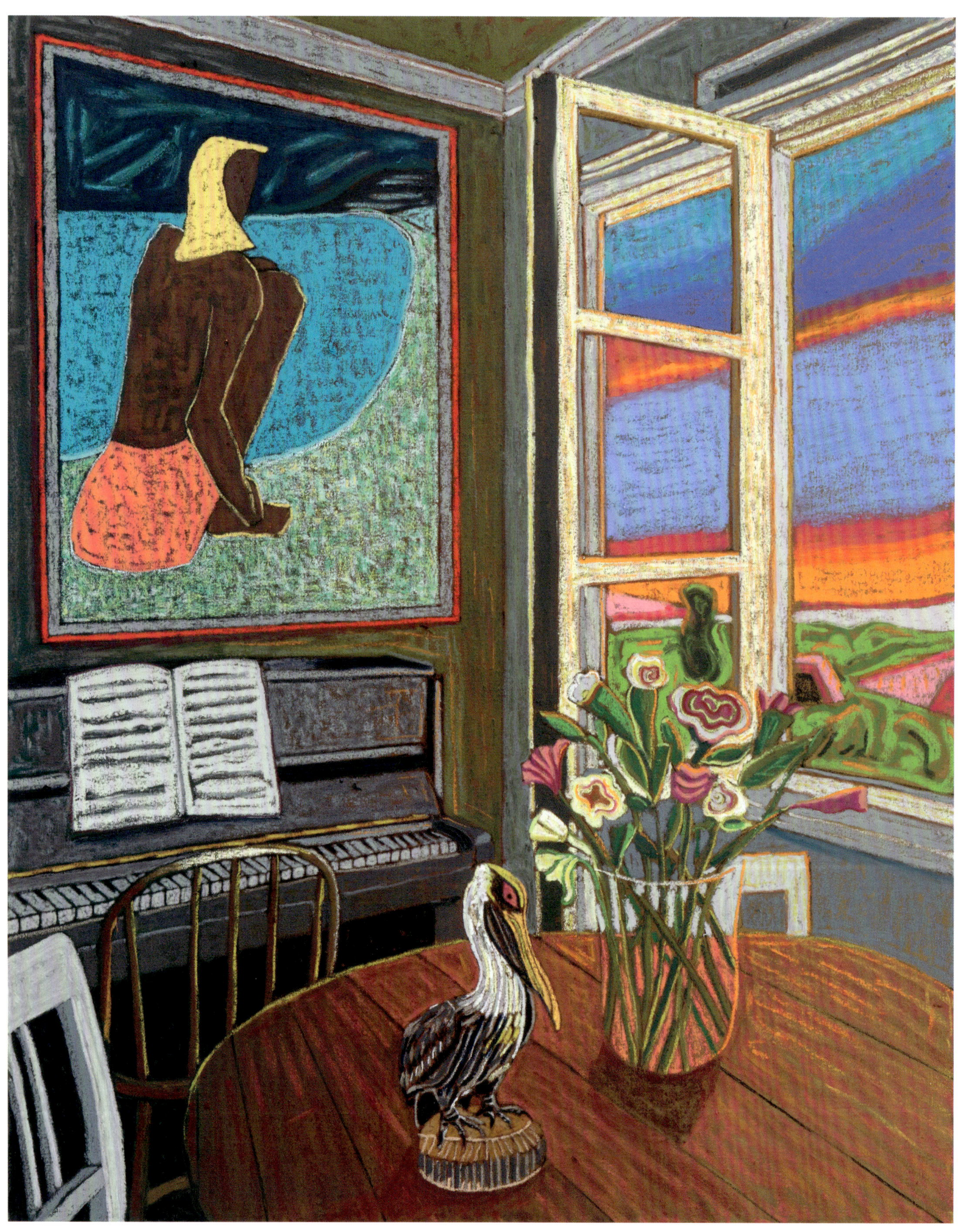

Ocean Side Apartment with Milton Avery, 2021, oil stick, oil pastel, and Flashe on linen, 60 x 50 inches

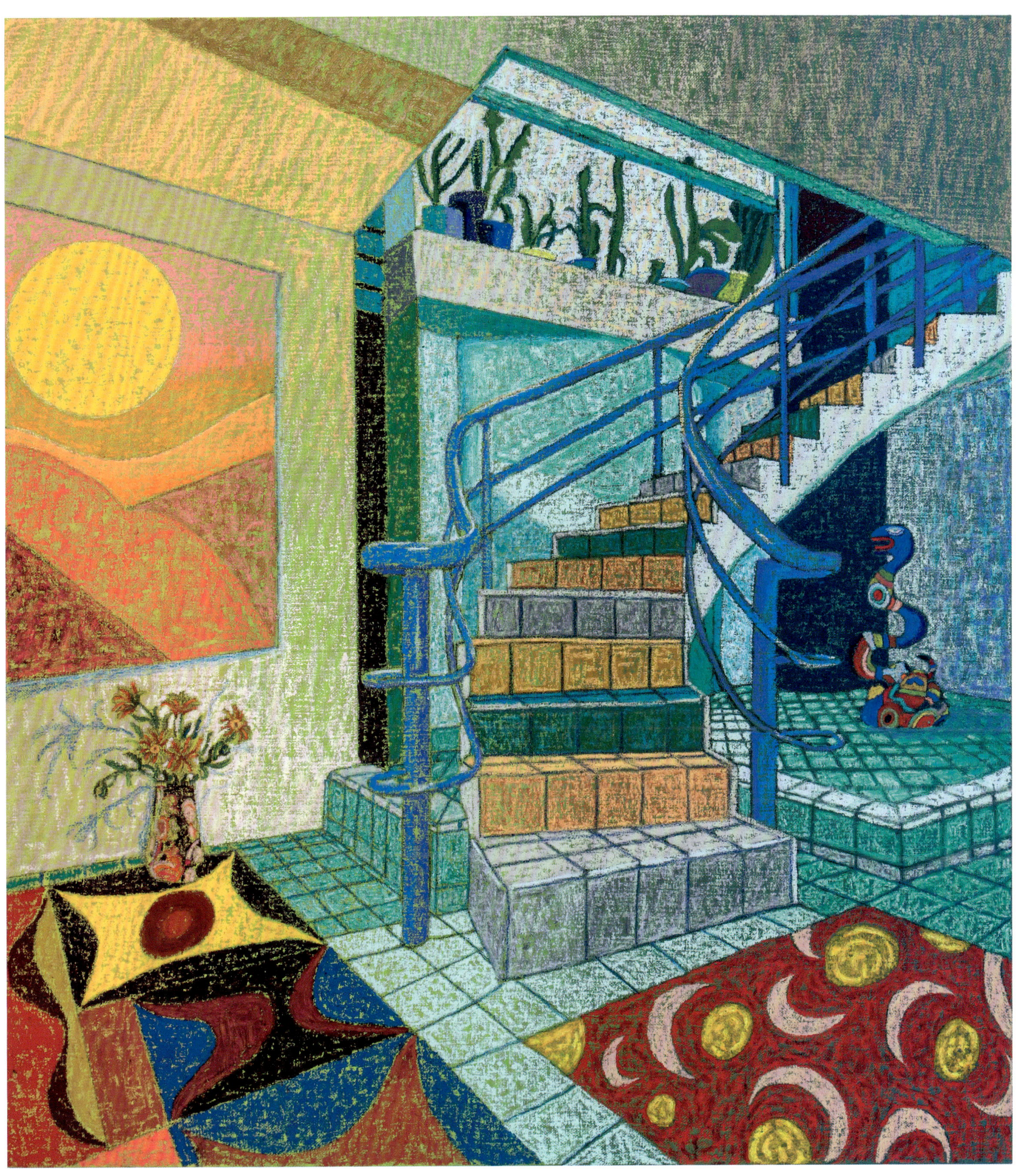

Interior with Niki de St. Phalle & Sophie Taeuber-Arp, 2021, oil stick, oil pastel, and Flashe on burlap over canvas, 78 ½ x 71 inches

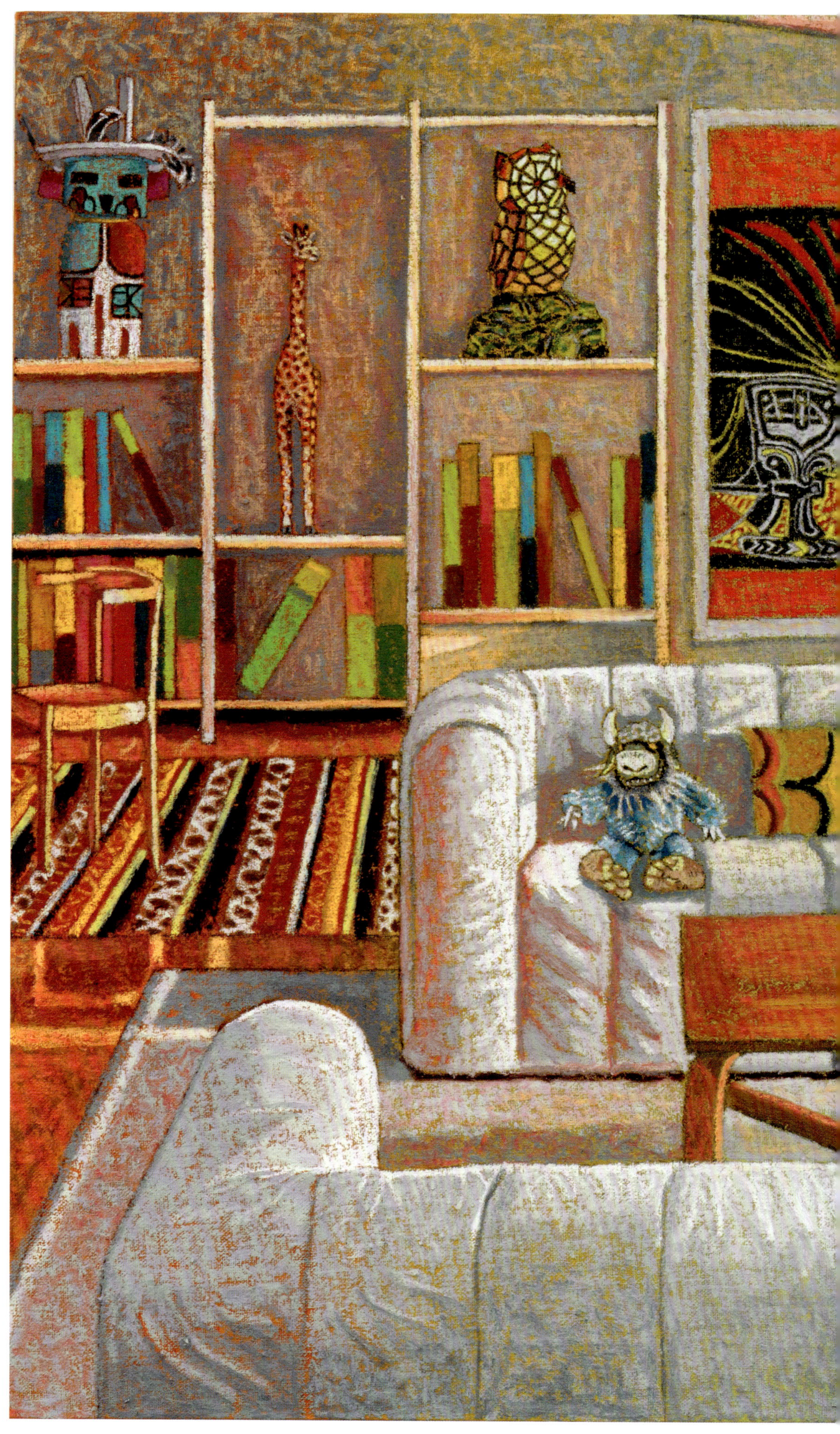

Interior with Picasso Print, Kachinas, & Wild Thing, 2023

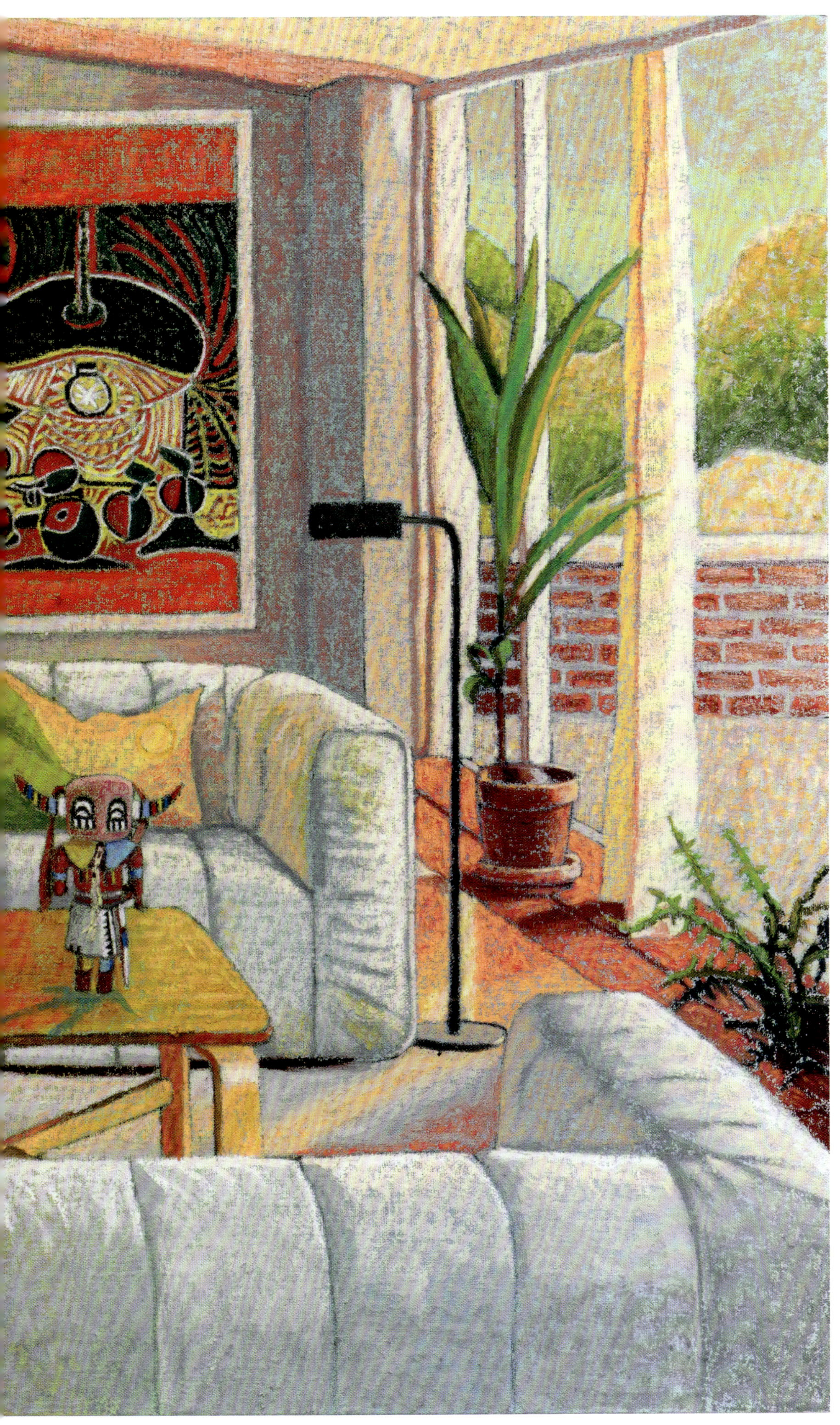

ck, oil pastel, and Flashe on burlap over canvas, 72 x 90 inches

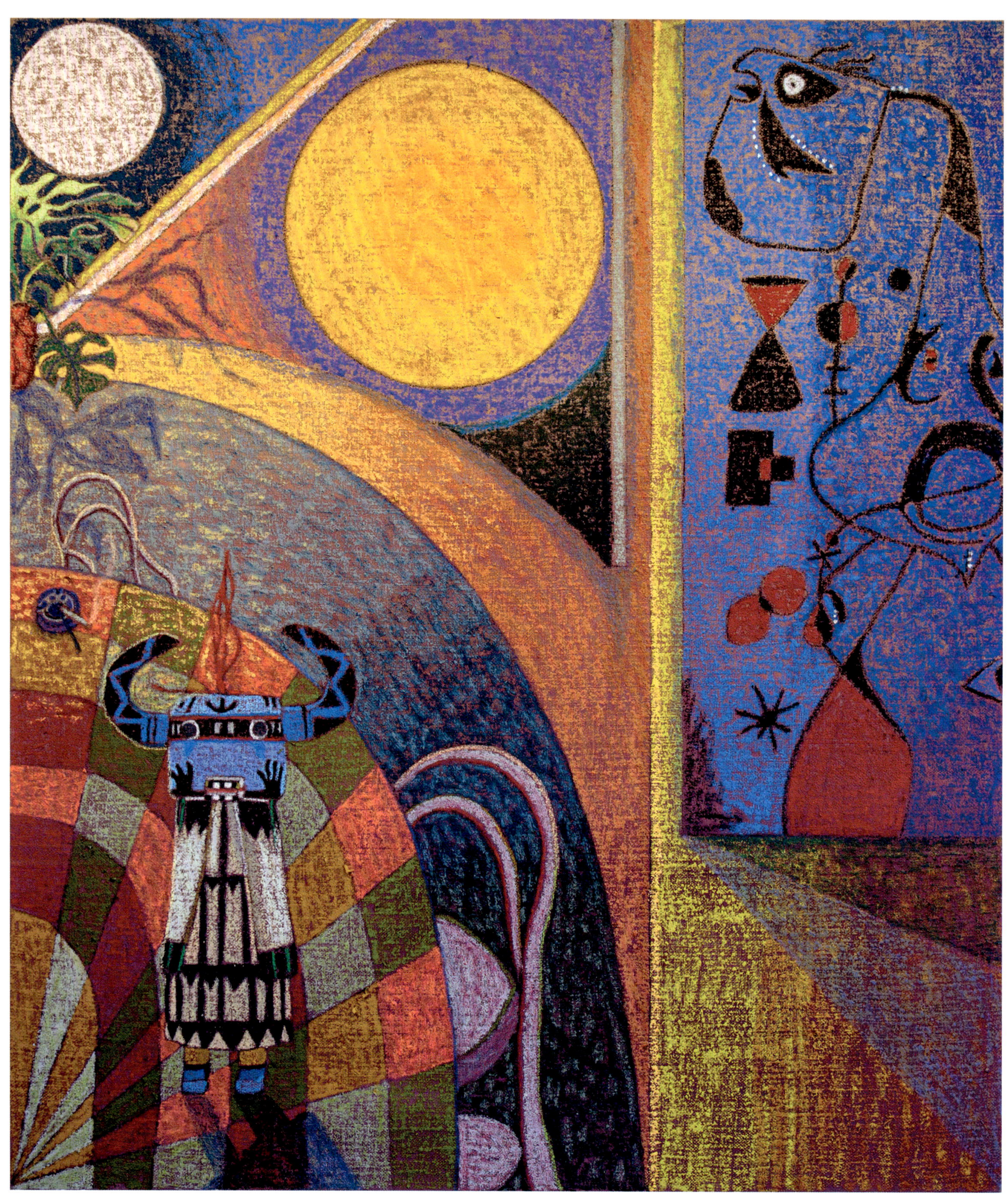

Moon & Sun / Interior with Kachina Doll & Joan Miró, 2020, oil stick, oil pastel, and Flashe on linen, 72 x 60 inches

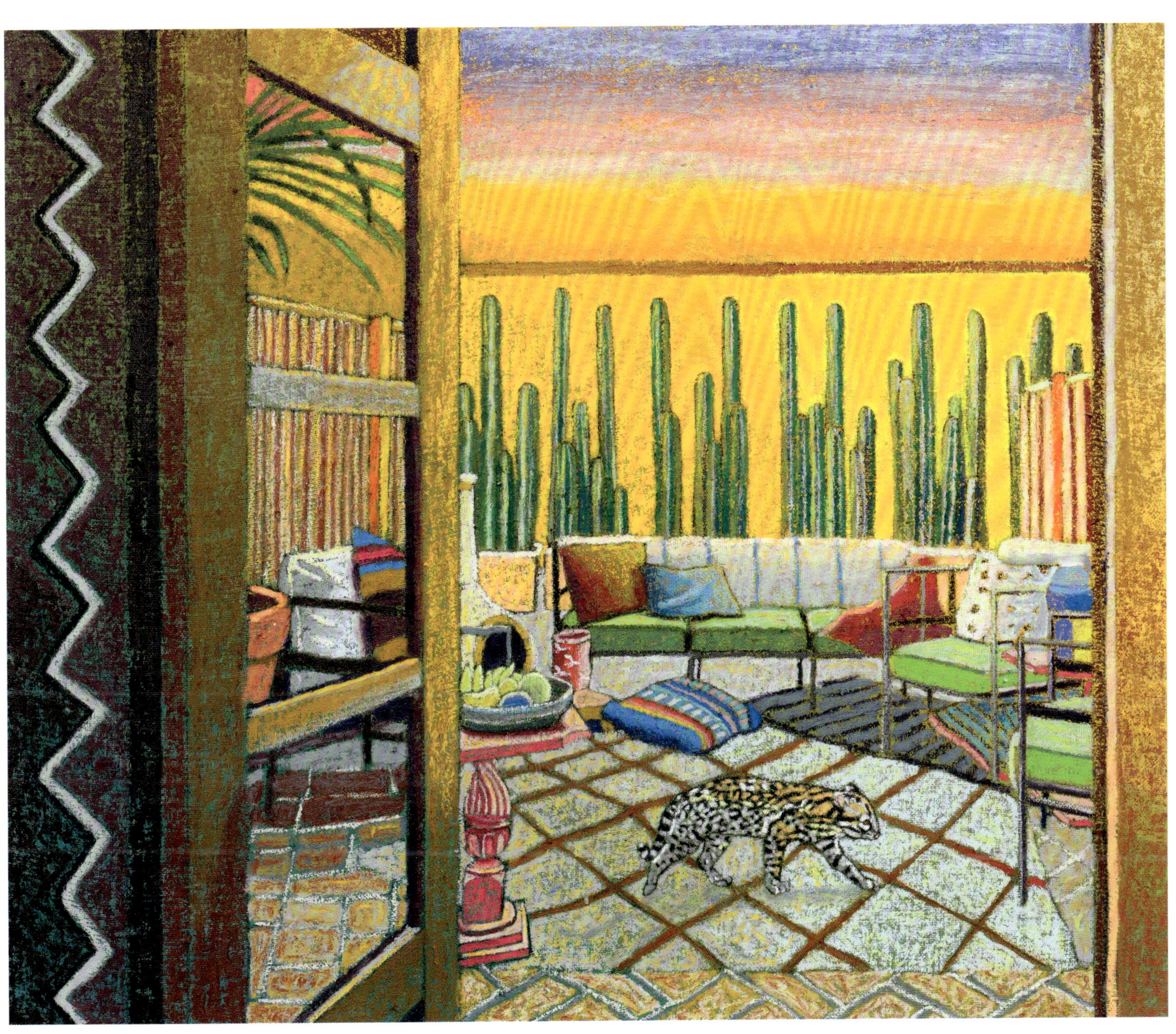

Sunset at Maison Hidalgo with Ocelot, 2023, oil stick, oil pastel, and Flashe on burlap over canvas, 50 x 60 inches

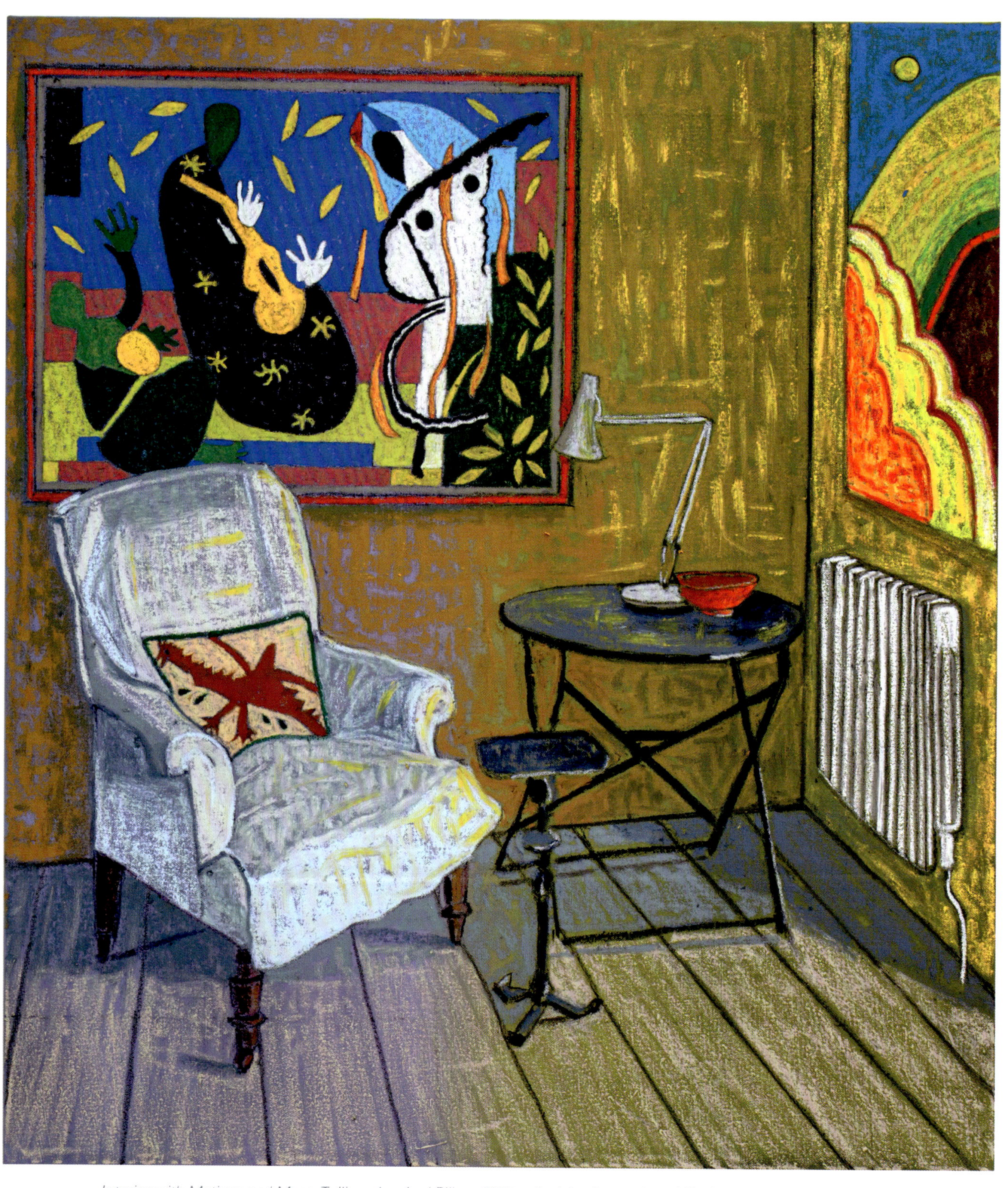

Interior with Matisse and Mose Tolliver–Inspired Pillow, 2021, oil stick, oil pastel, and Flashe on linen, 46 x 41 inches

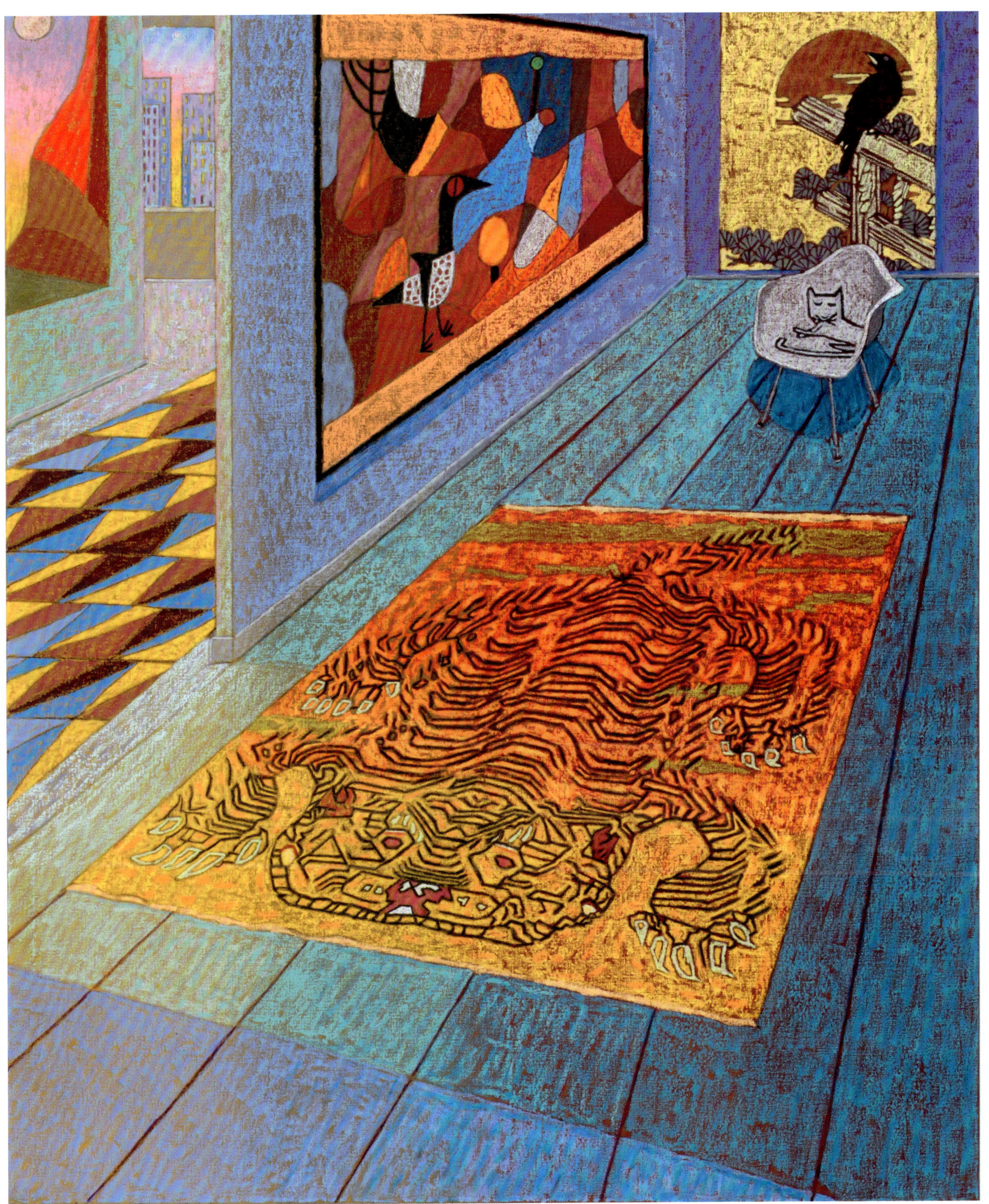

Interior with Tibetan Rug & Paul Klee Tapestry, 2020, oil stick, oil pastel, and Flashe on linen, 84 x 68 inches

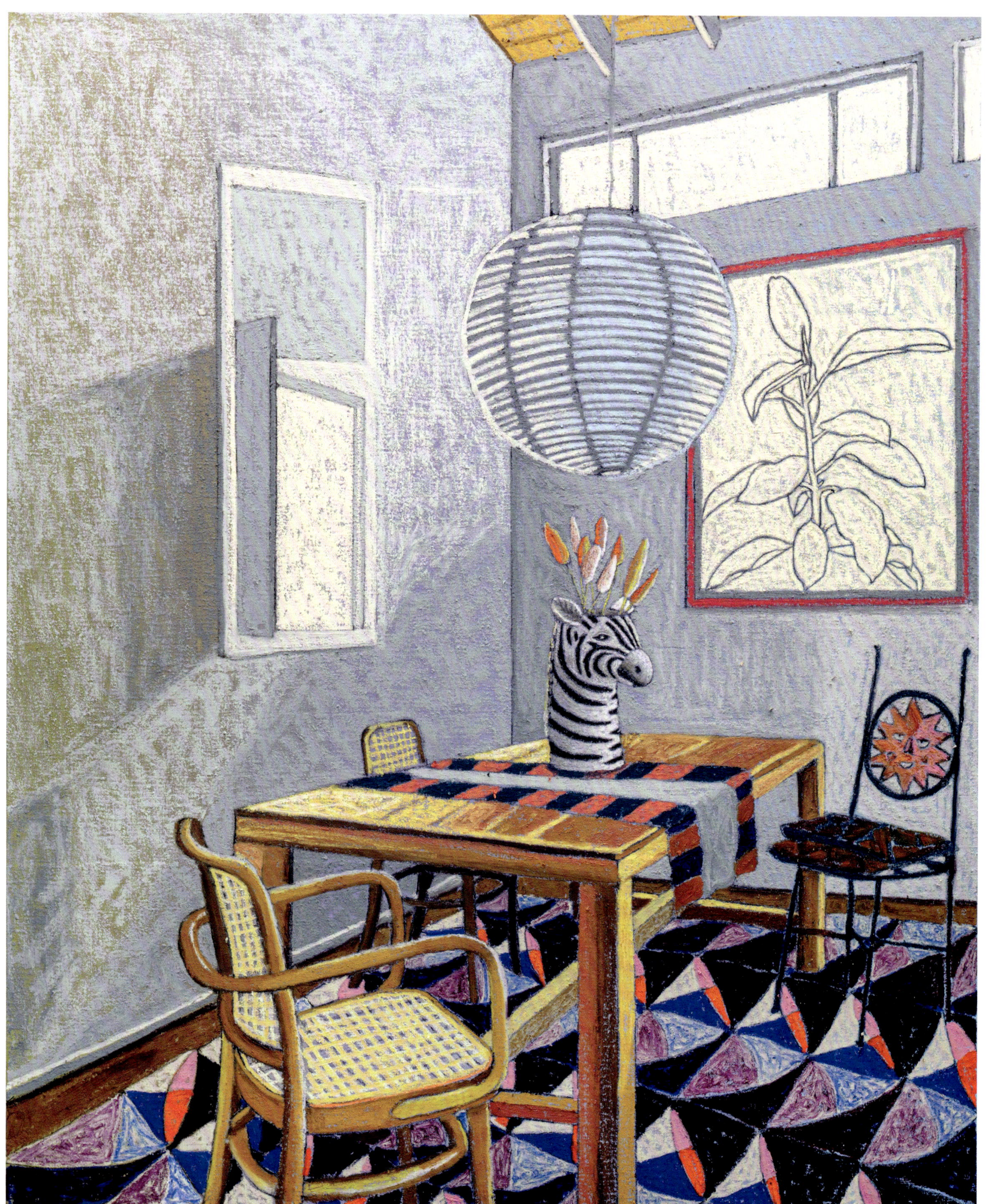

Interior with Zebra Vase & Ellsworth Kelly, 2022, oil stick, oil pastel, and Flashe on burlap over canvas, 72 x 60 inches

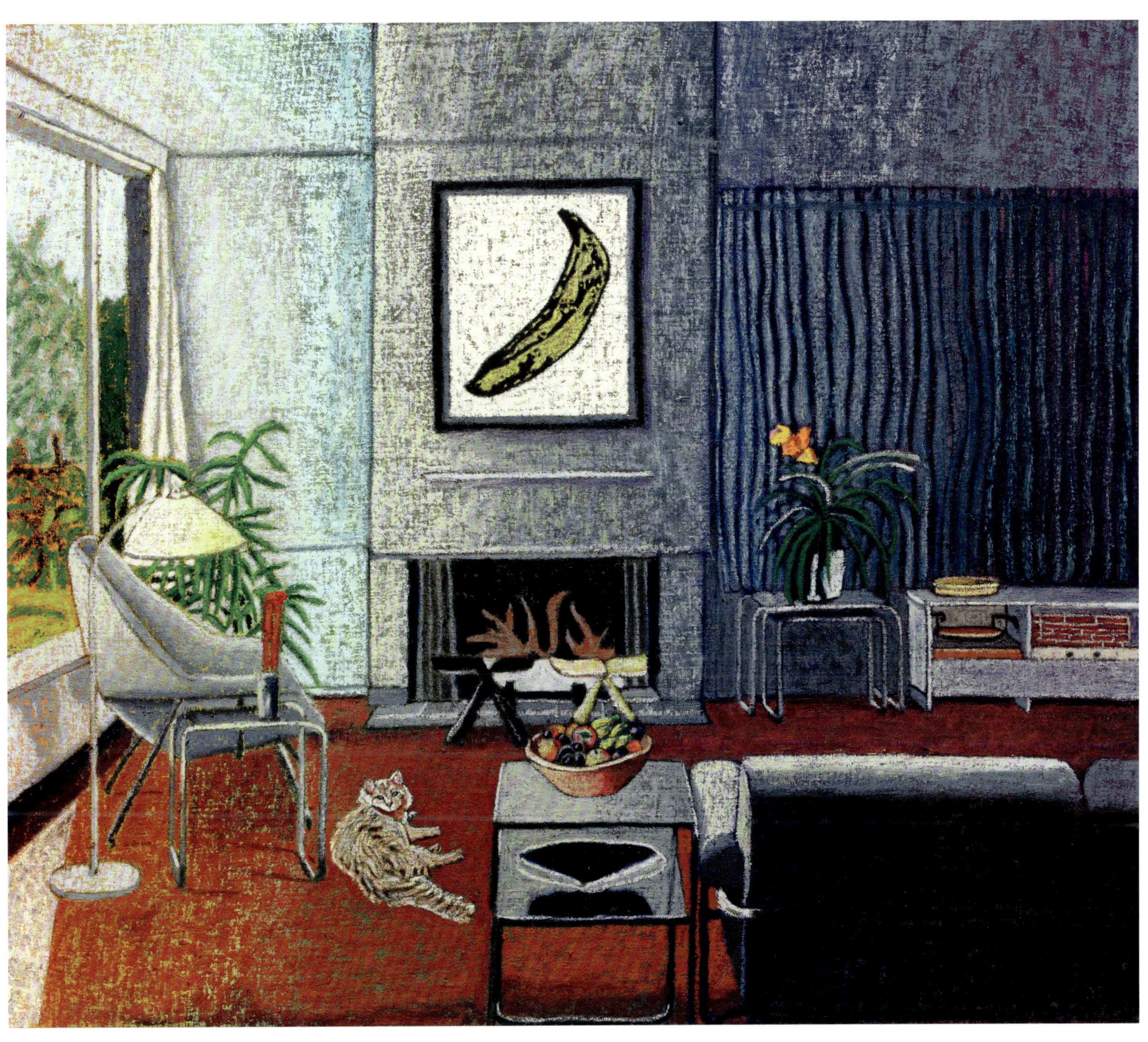

Walter Gropius Interior with Andy Warhol, 2022, oil stick, oil pastel, and Flashe on burlap over canvas, 72 x 84 inches

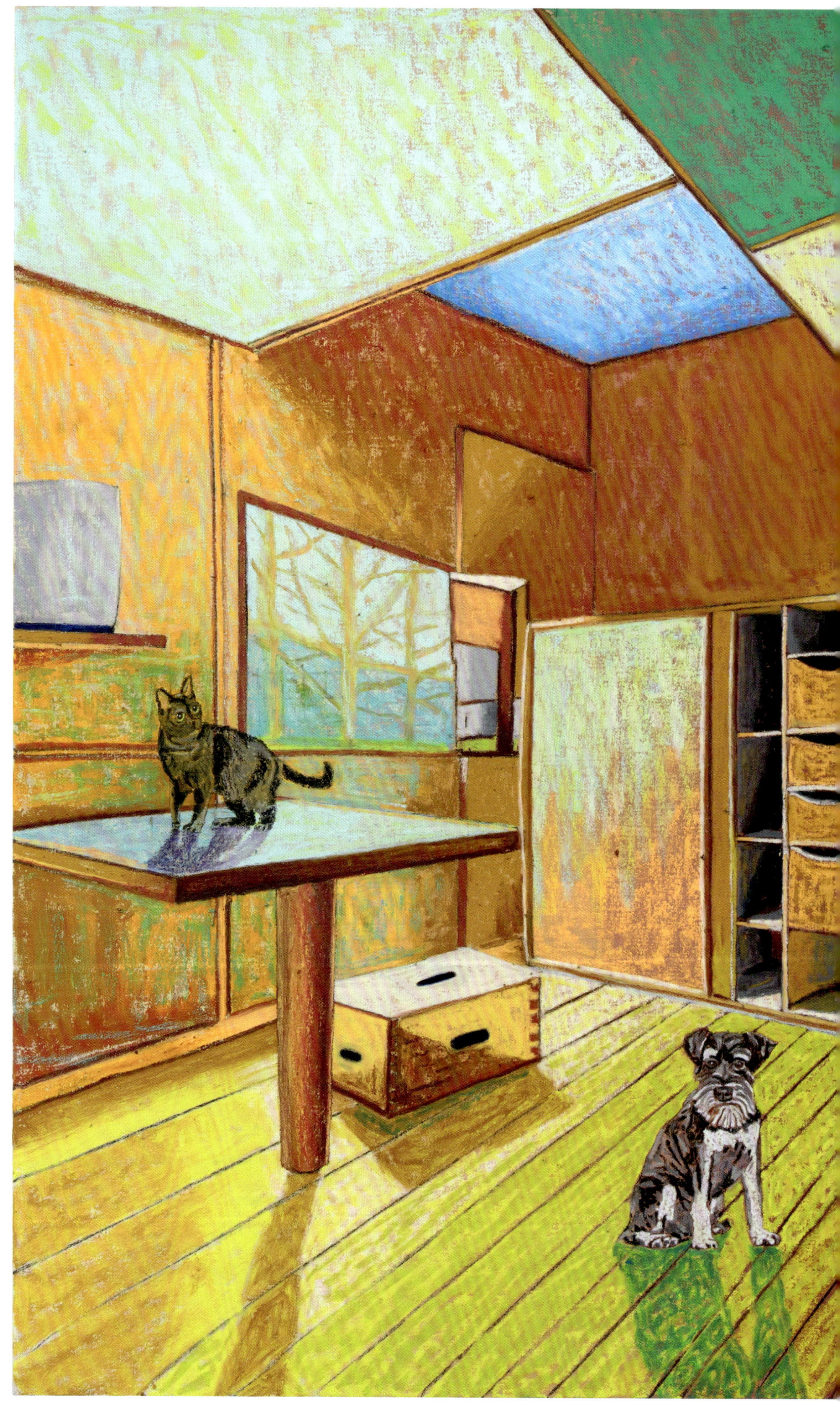

Corbusier Interior with Schnauzer & Black Cats, 20

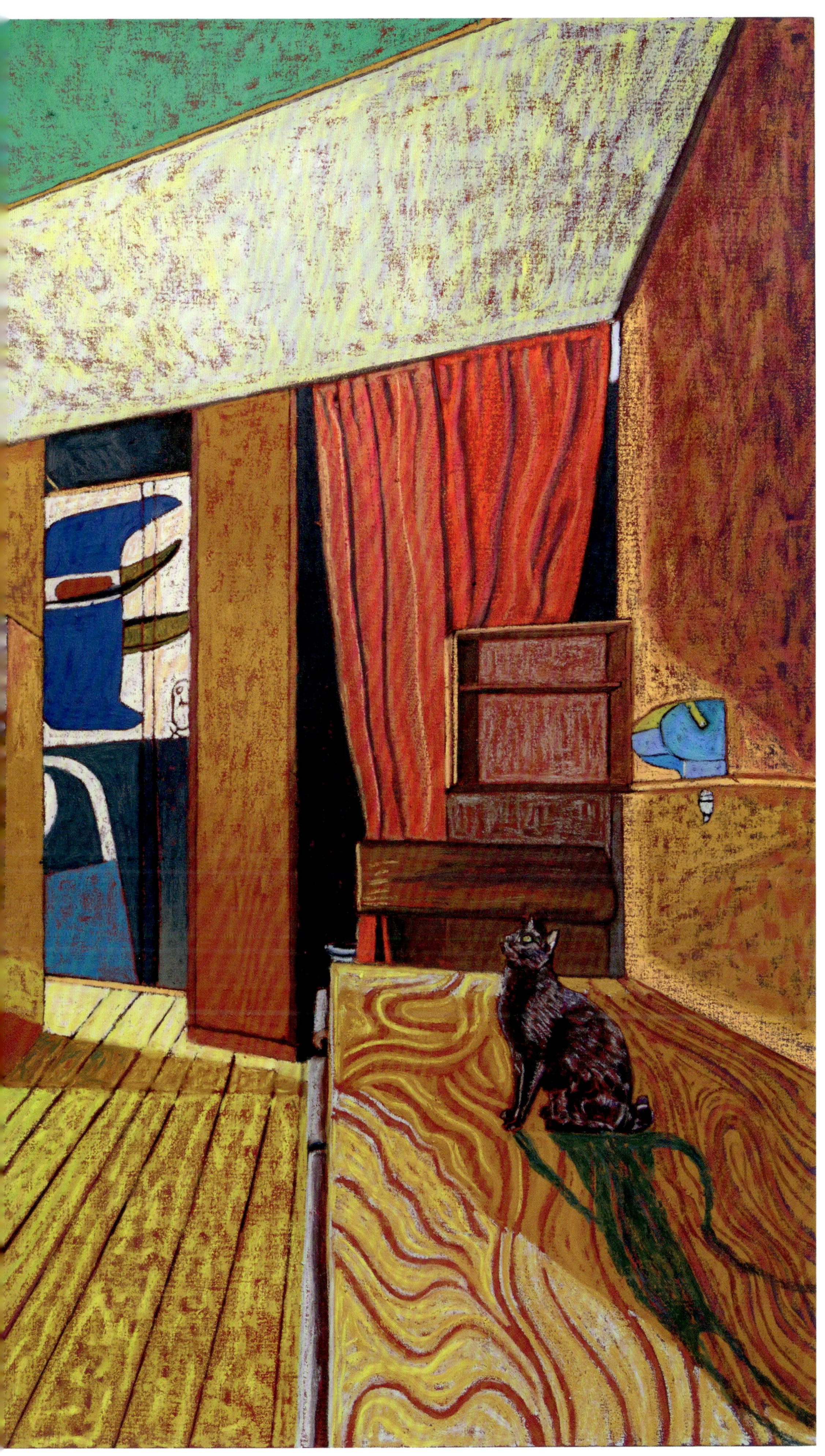

stick, oil pastel, and Flashe on linen, 90 x 112 inches

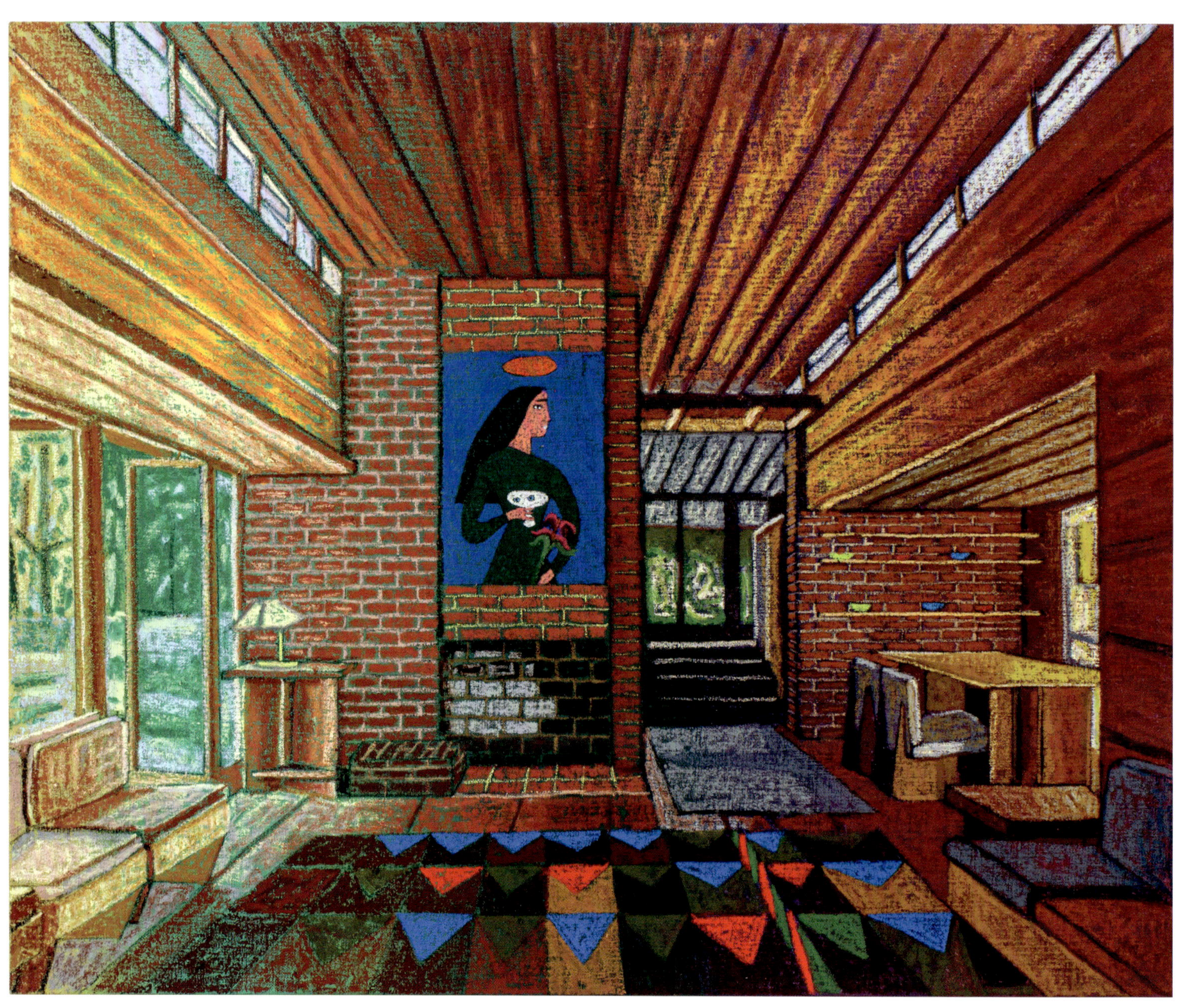

Alfredo Volpi–Inspired Tapestry in a Frank Lloyd Wright Interior, 2021, oil stick, oil pastel, and Flashe on burlap over canvas, 72 x 84 inches

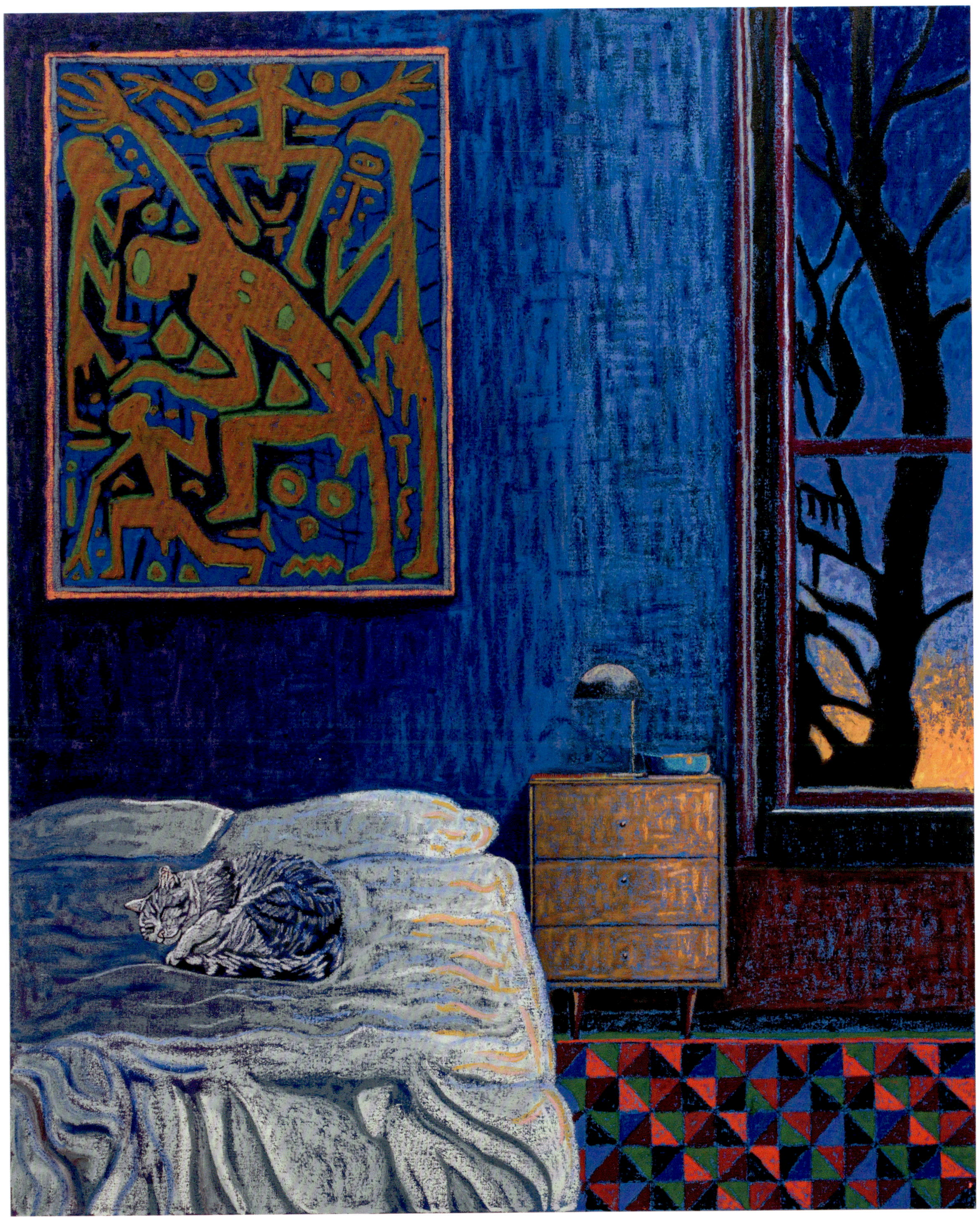

Bedroom with A.R. Penck, 2021, oil stick, oil pastel, and Flashe on linen, 70 x 62 inches

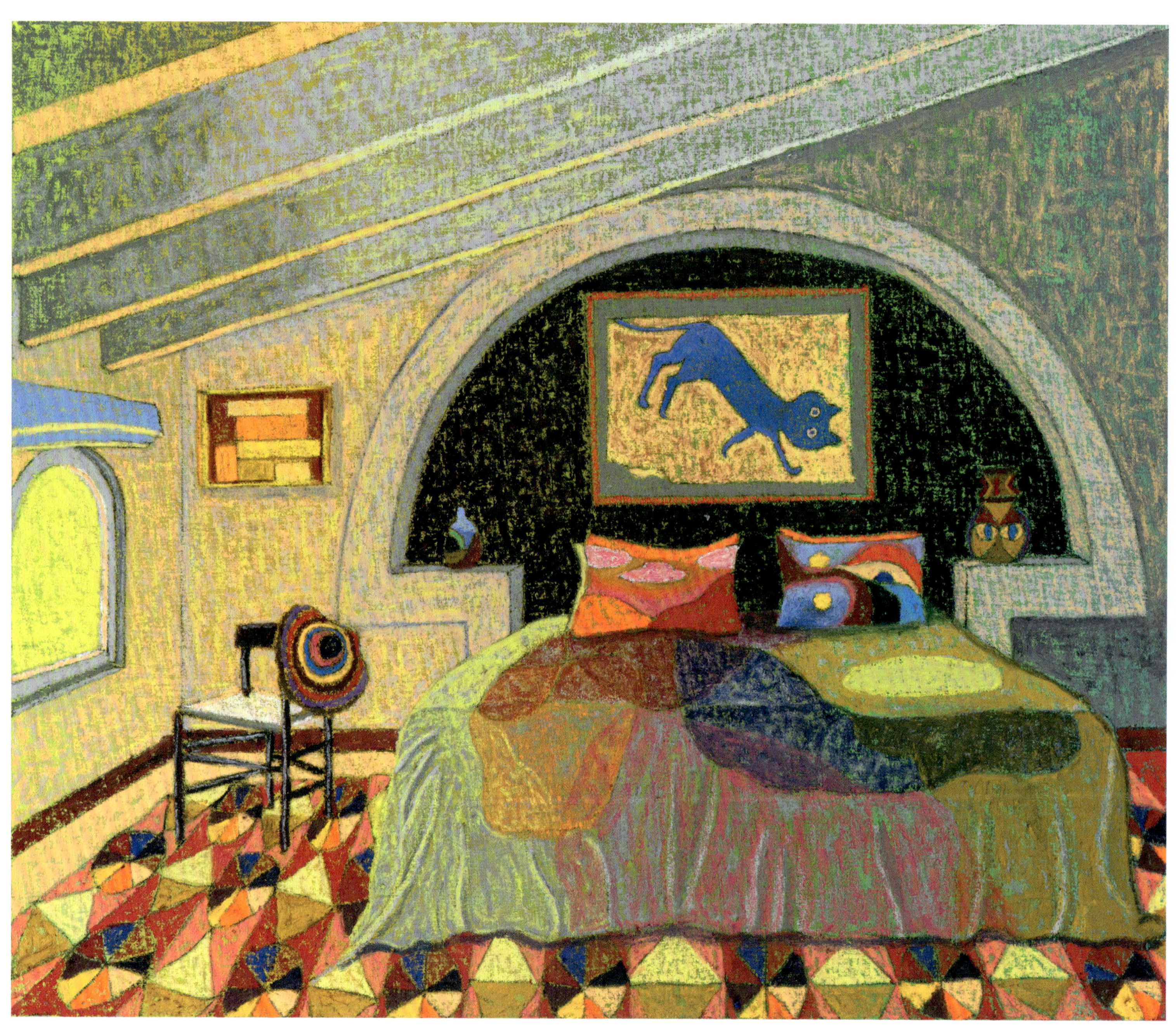

Cadmium Sunlit Bedroom with Bill Traylor & Nancy Shaver, 2022, oil stick, oil pastel, and Flashe on burlap over canvas, 60 x 72 inches

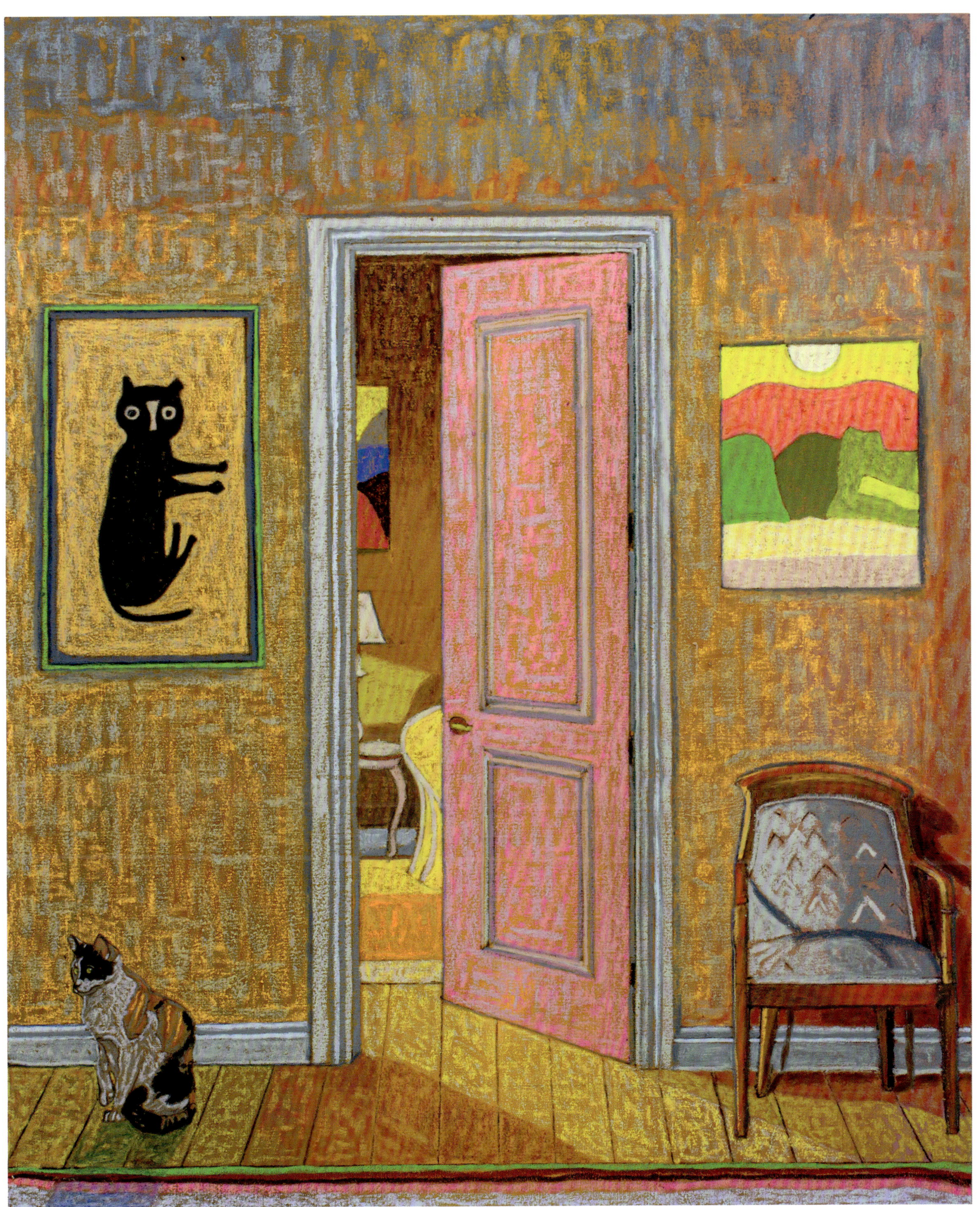

Interior with Bill Traylor & Etel Adnan, 2021, oil stick, oil pastel, and Flashe on linen, 72 x 60 inches

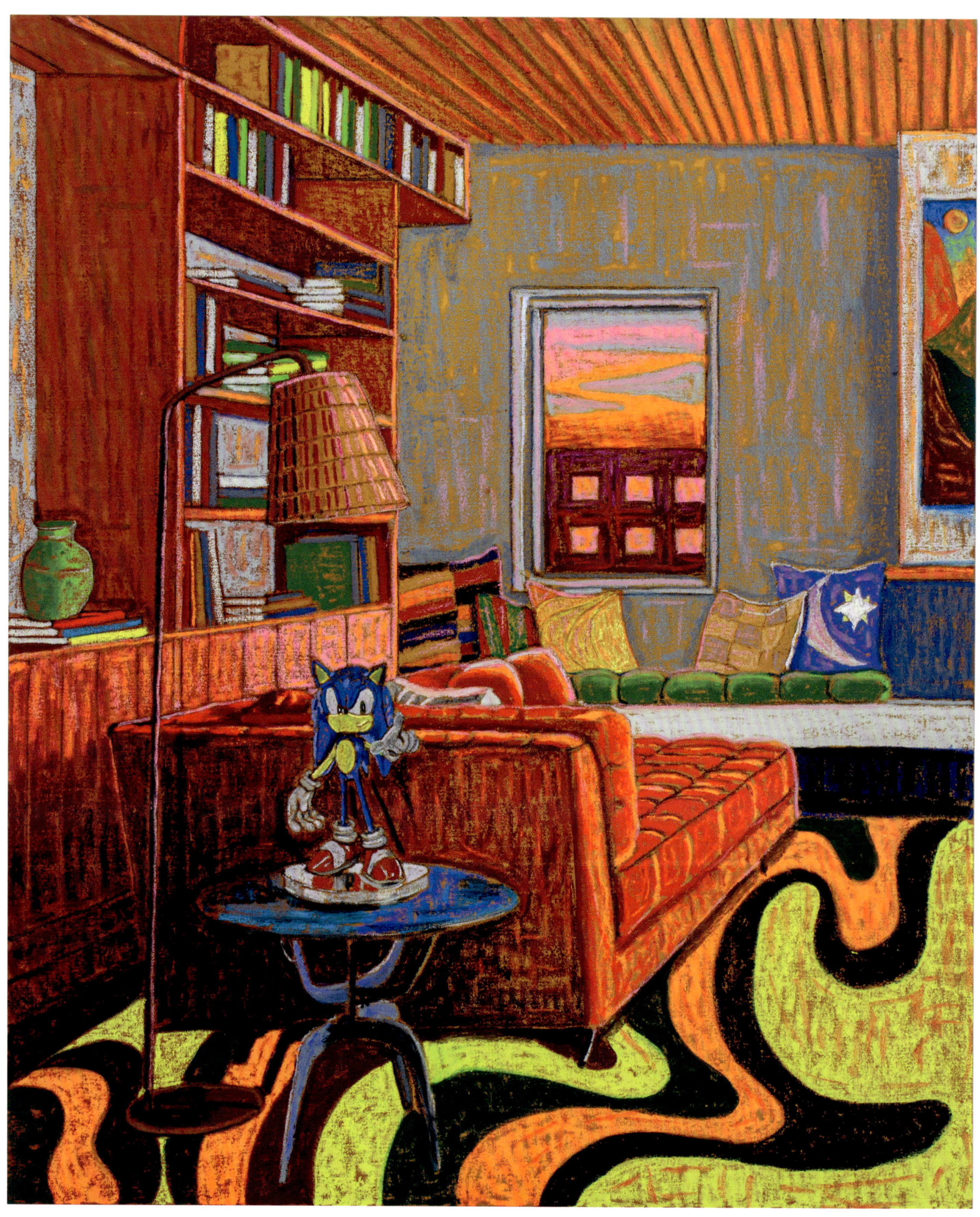

Interior with Sonic & JJ Manford Rug, 2021, oil stick, oil pastel, and Flashe on linen, 72 x 60 inches

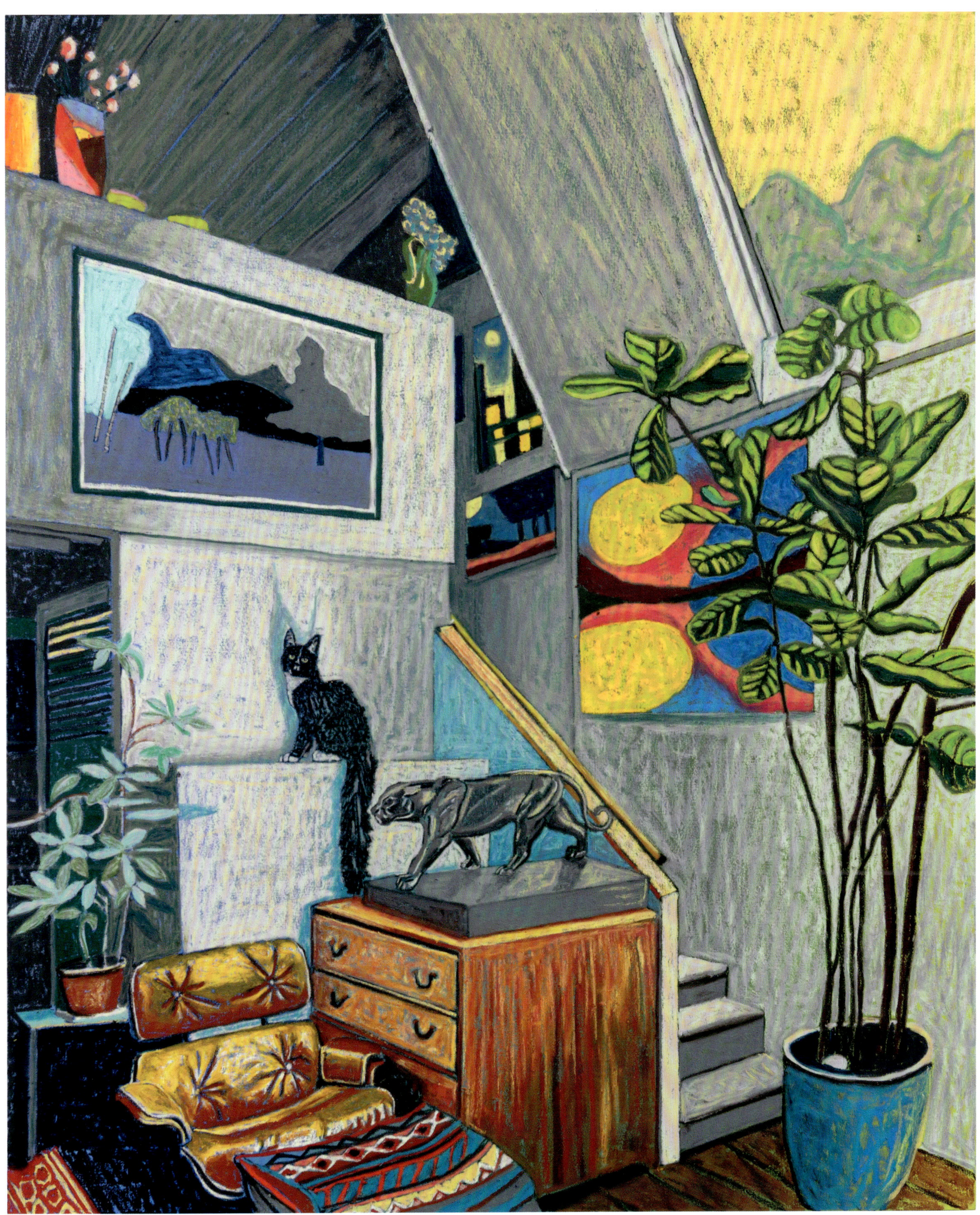

New York City Interior with Milton Avery & Panther, 2022, oil stick, oil pastel, and Flashe on linen, 84 x 72 inches

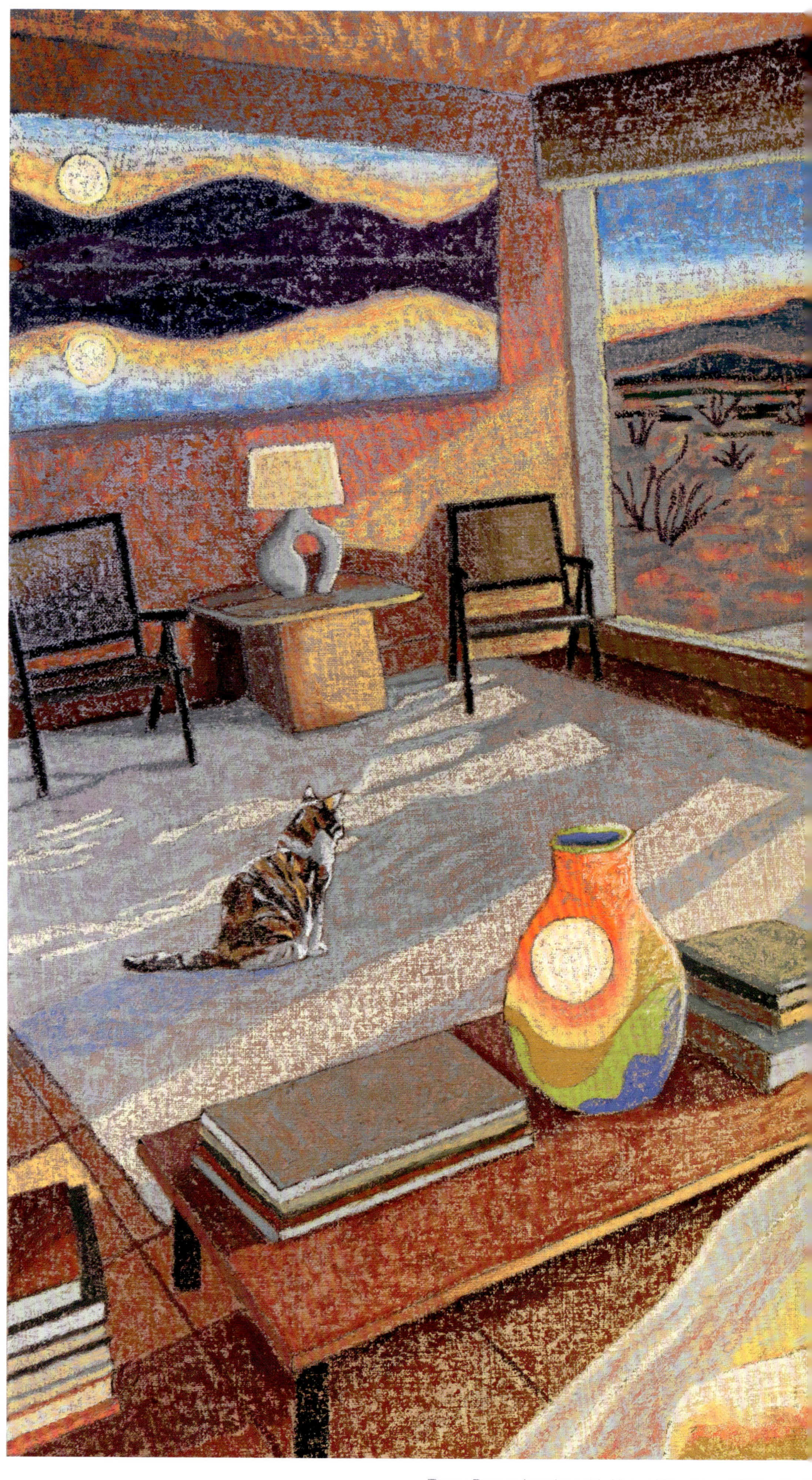

Texas Desert Interior with Noguchi Lantern, 2023, oil sti

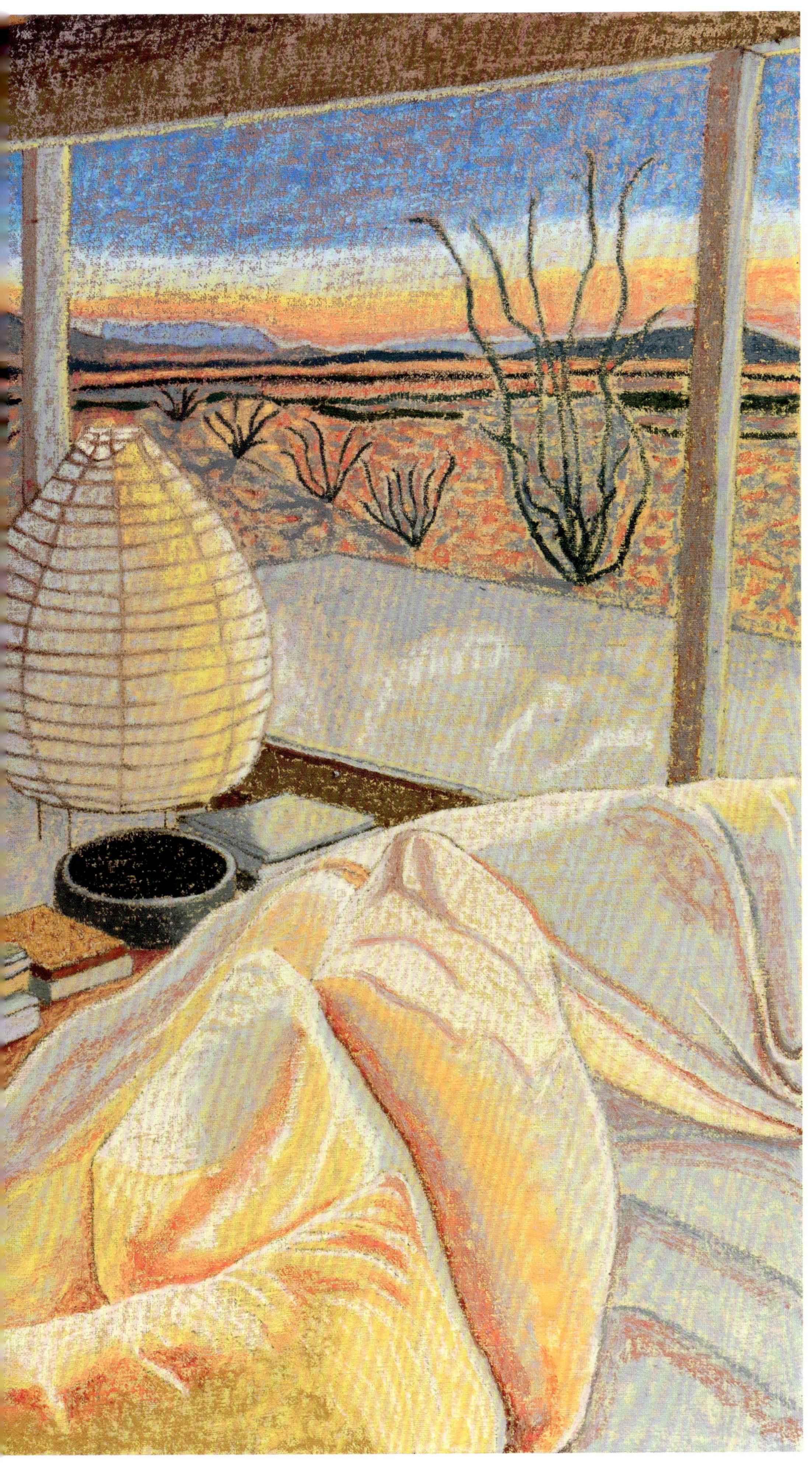

pastel, and Flashe on burlap over canvas, 72 x 84 inches

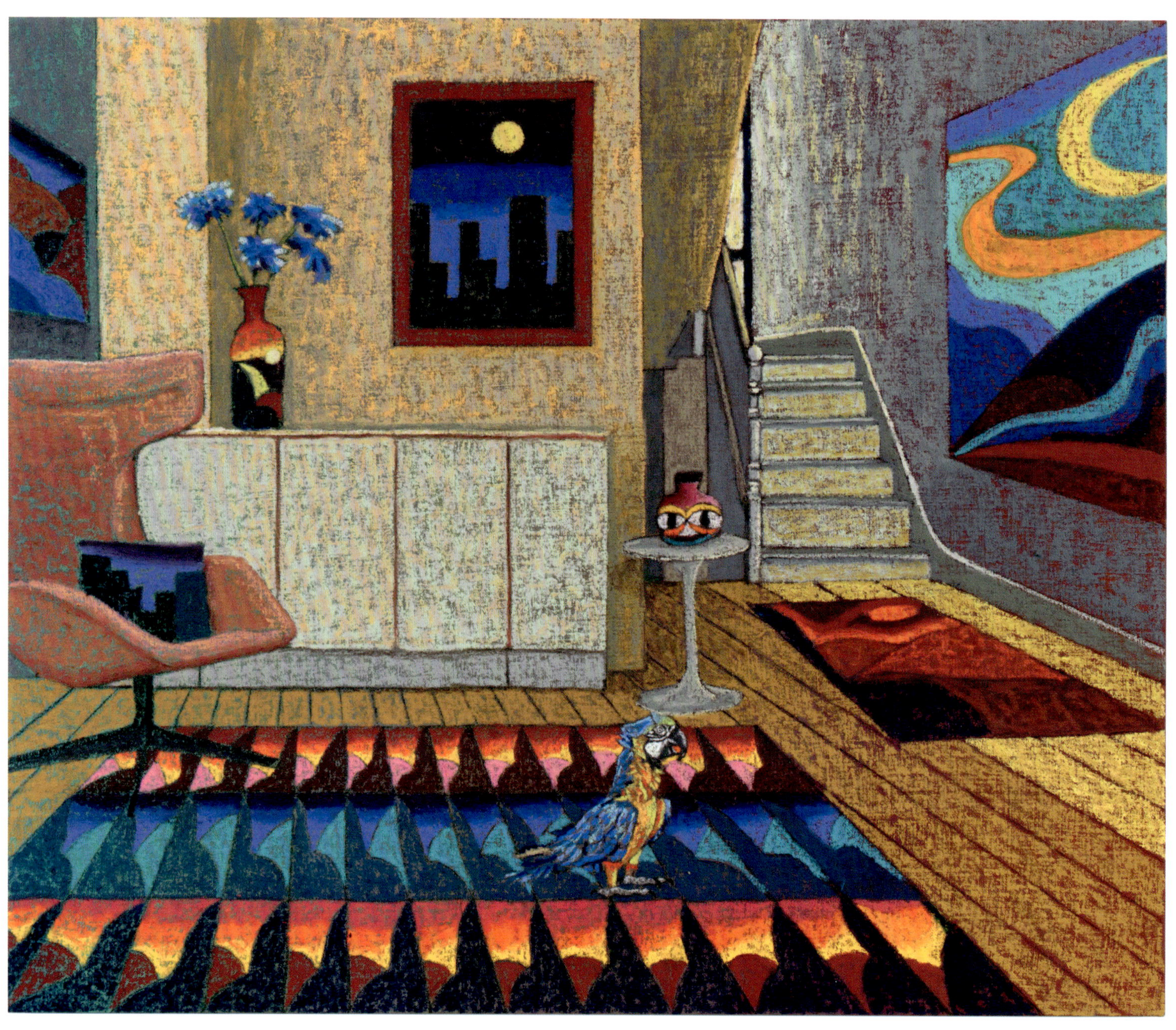

Interior with Parrot & City Painting, 2022, oil stick, oil pastel, and Flashe on burlap over canvas, 72 x 84 inches

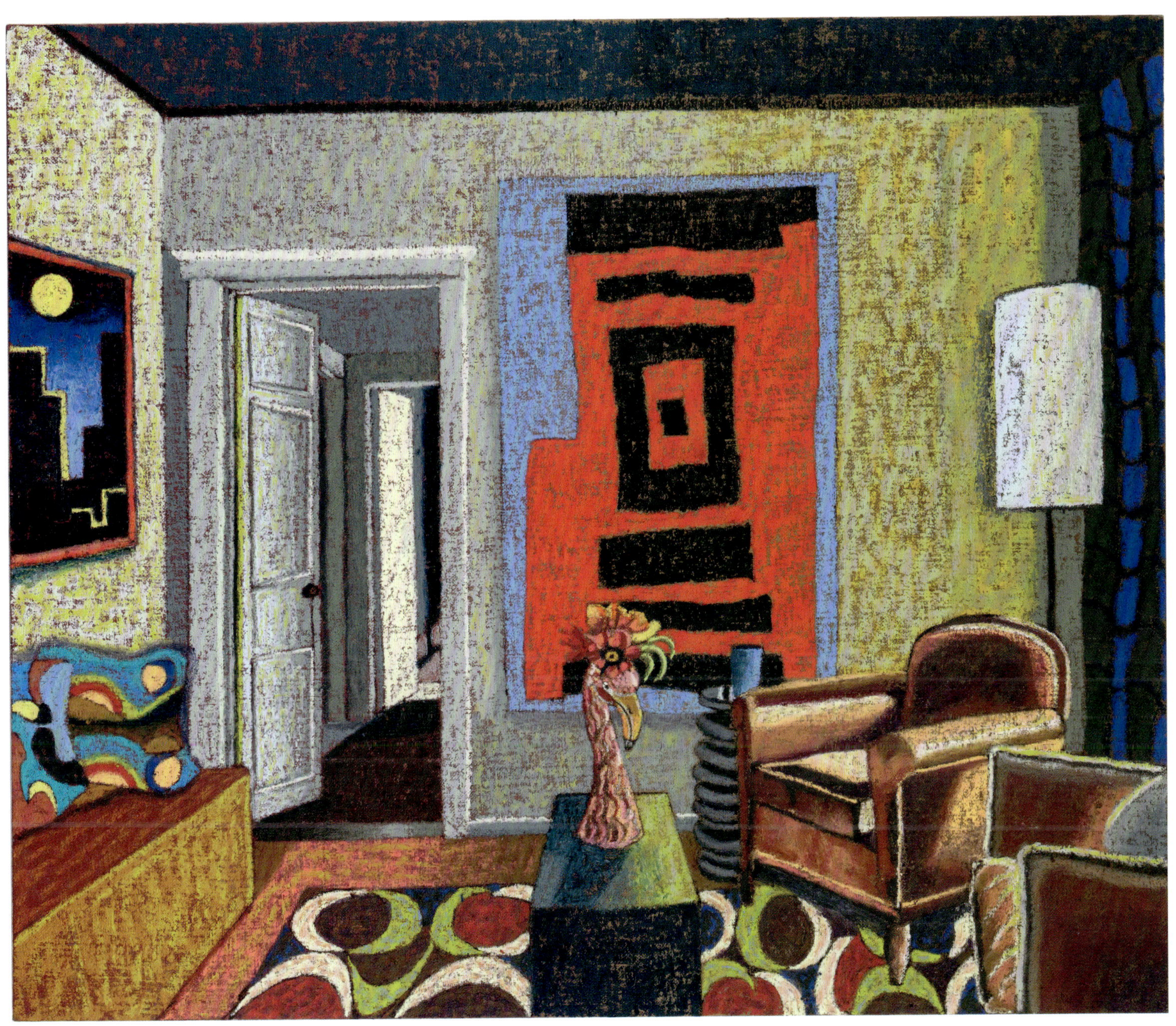

Interior with Gee's Bend Quilt & Flamingo Vase, 2022, oil stick, oil pastel, and Flashe on burlap over canvas, 60 x 72 inches

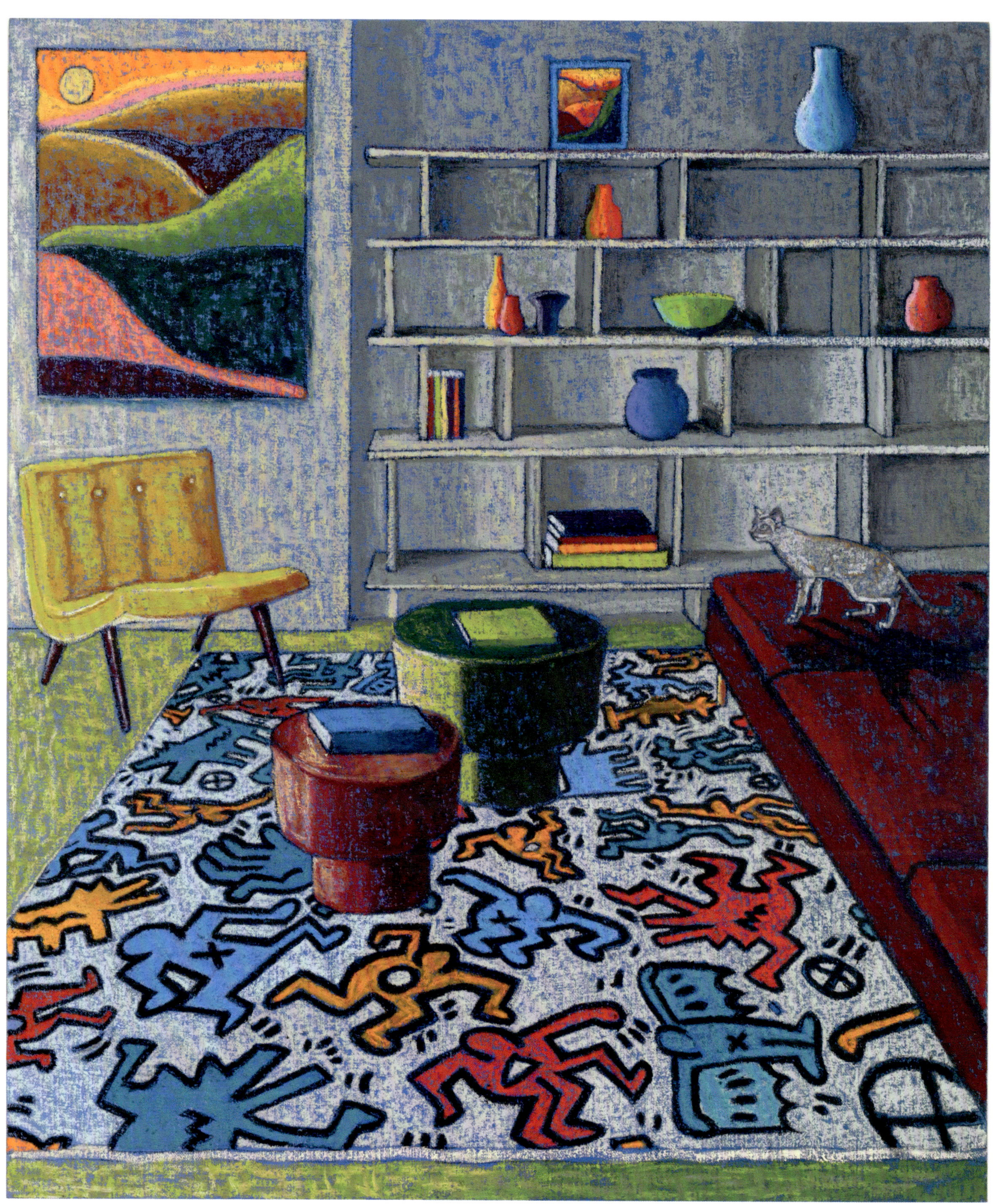

Interior with Keith Haring Rug & Siamese Cat, 2022, oil stick, oil pastel, and Flashe on burlap over canvas, 84 x 72 inches

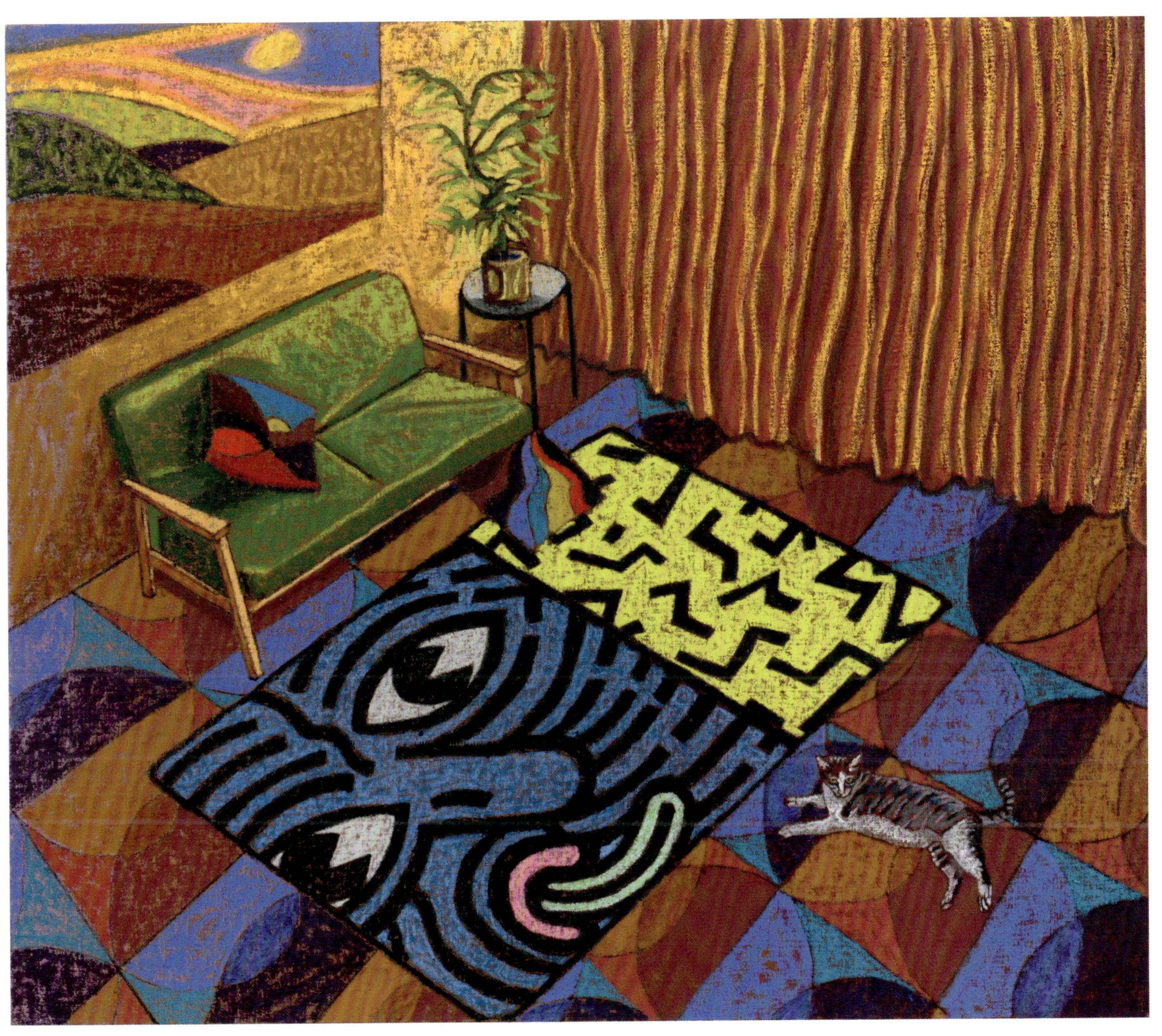

Interior with Keith Haring Rug & JJ Manford Floor Tiles, 2022, oil stick, oil pastel, and Flashe on burlap over canvas, 72 x 84 inches

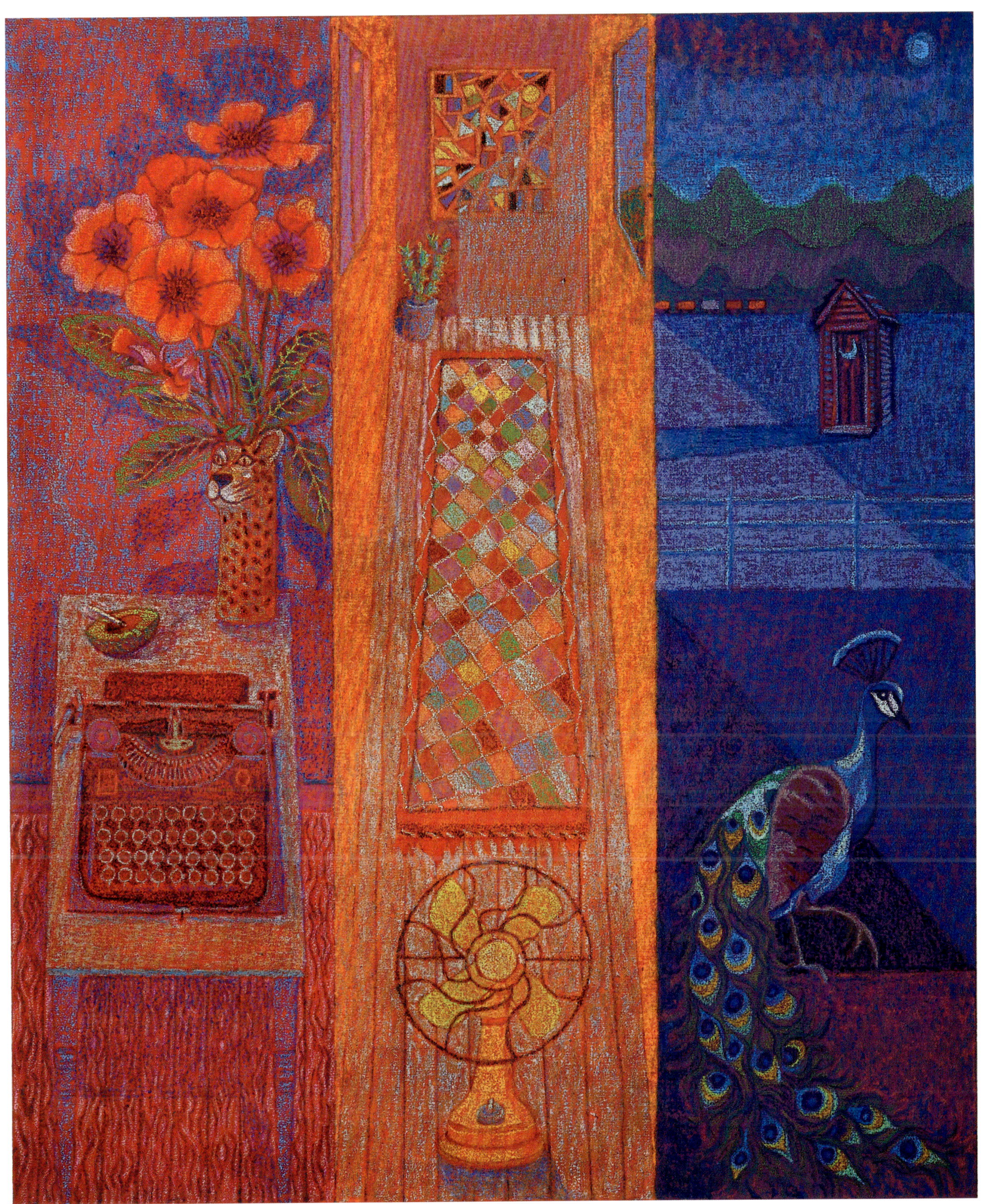

Exotic Heat/Summer Birds, 2020, oil stick, oil pastel, and Flashe on burlap over canvas, 72 x 61 inches

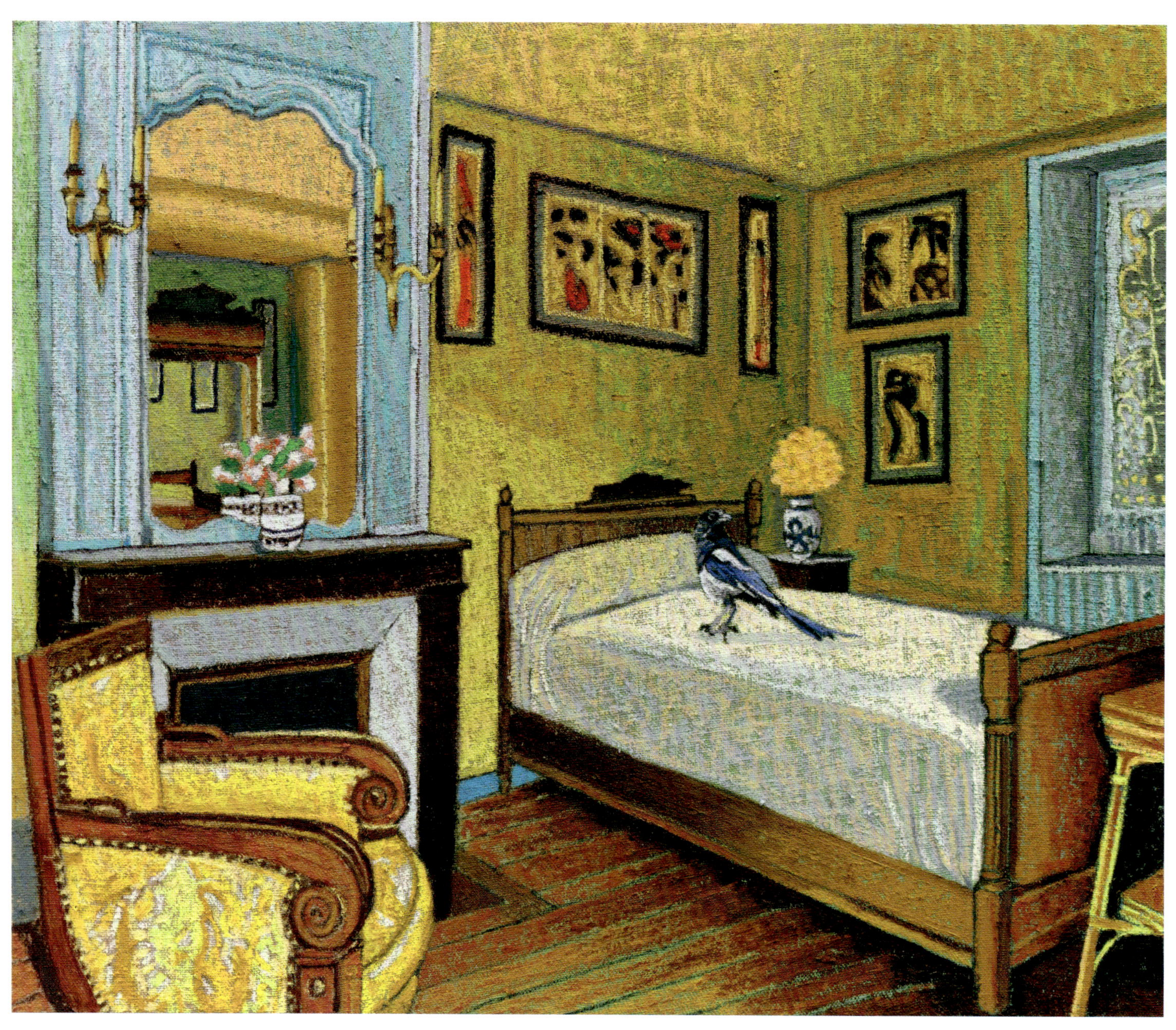

Monet's Bedroom at Giverny, 2023, oil stick, oil pastel, and Flashe on burlap over canvas, 50 x 60 inches

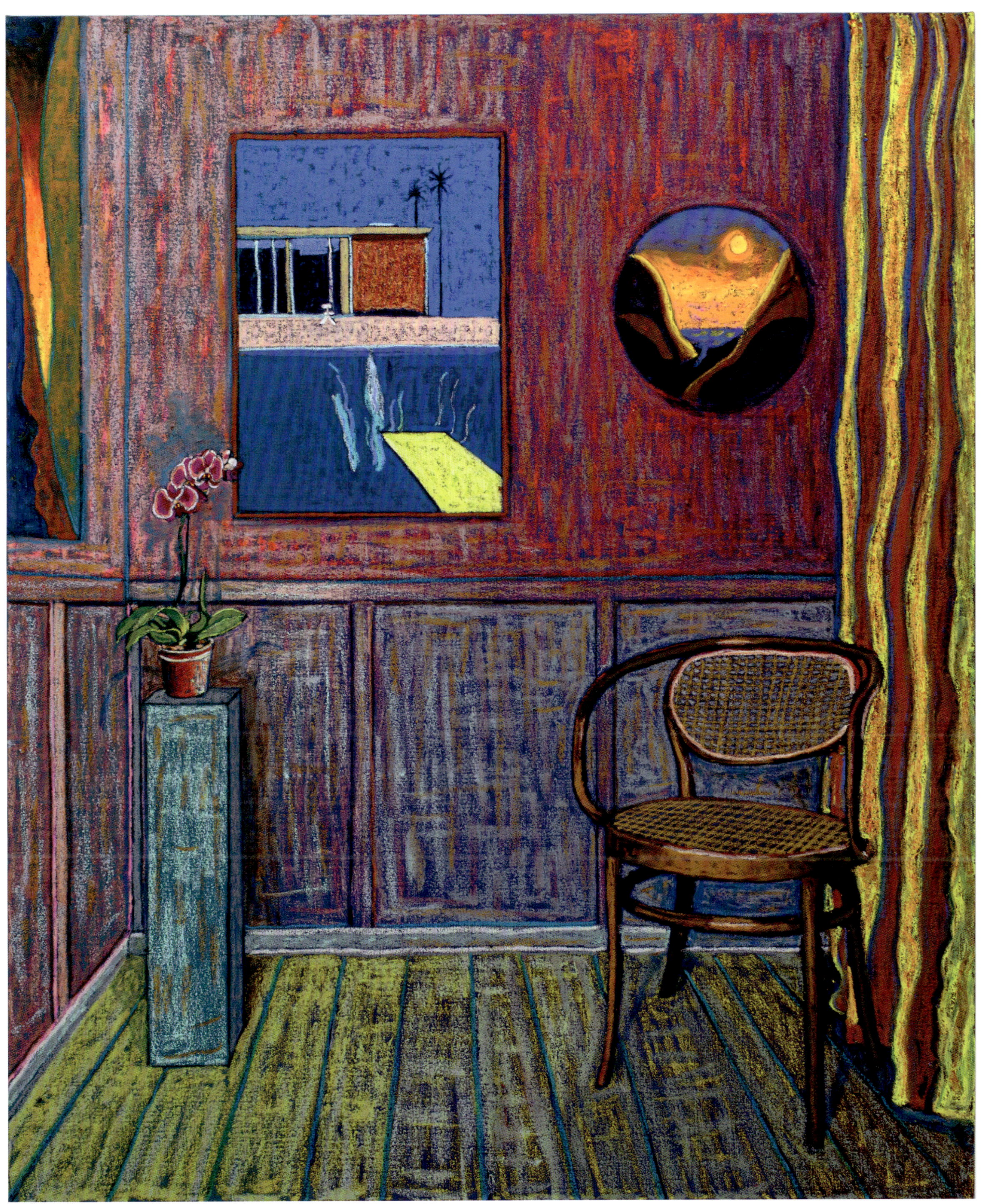

Interior with David Hockney Print & Bentwood Chair, 2021, oil stick, oil pastel, and Flashe on linen, 72 x 60 inches

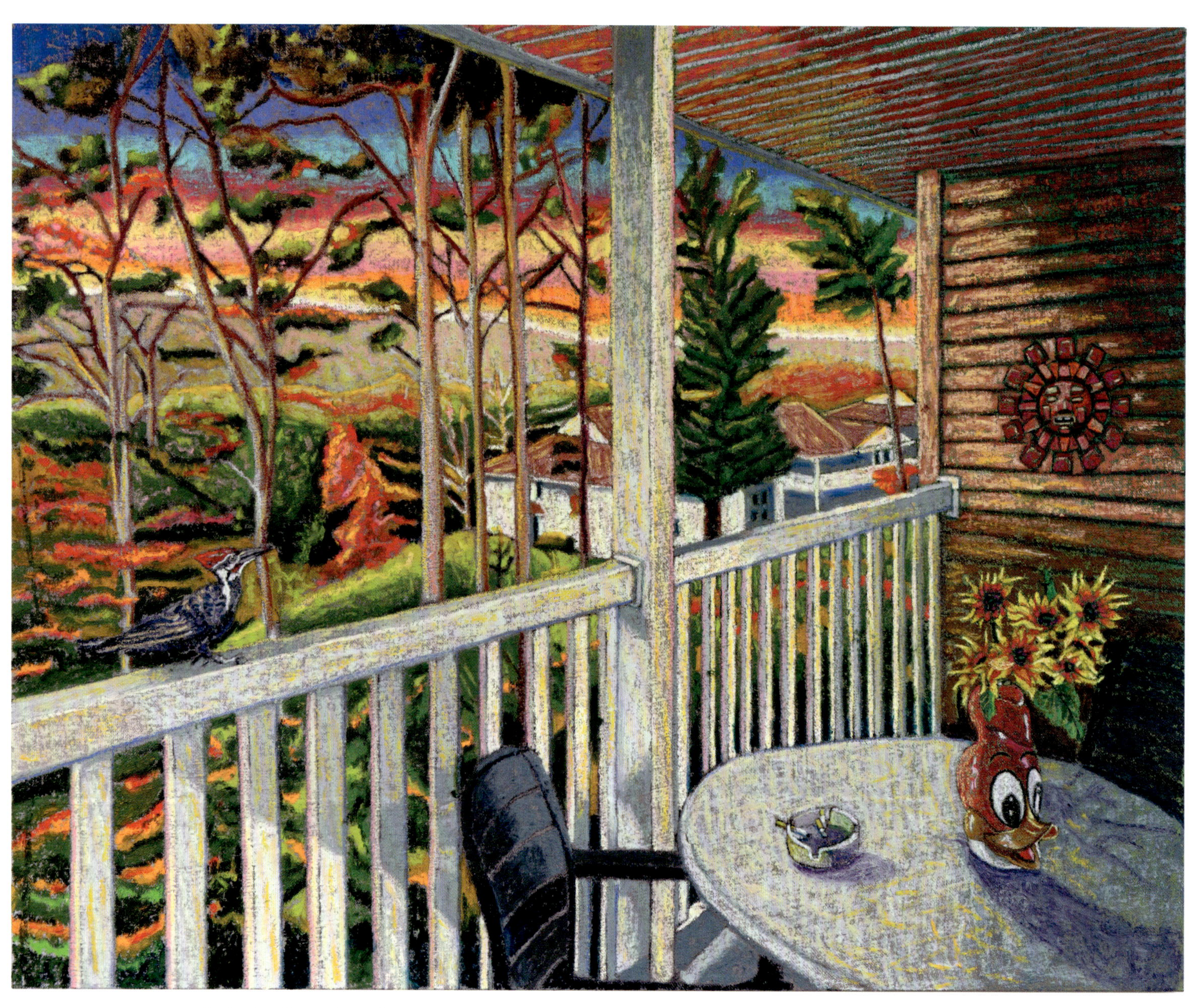

Berkshires Porch Scene (Porch with Woodpecker, Woodie the Woodpecker Vase, & Steve Keister Sun), 2023,
oil stick, oil pastel, and Flashe on burlap over canvas, 72 x 90 inches

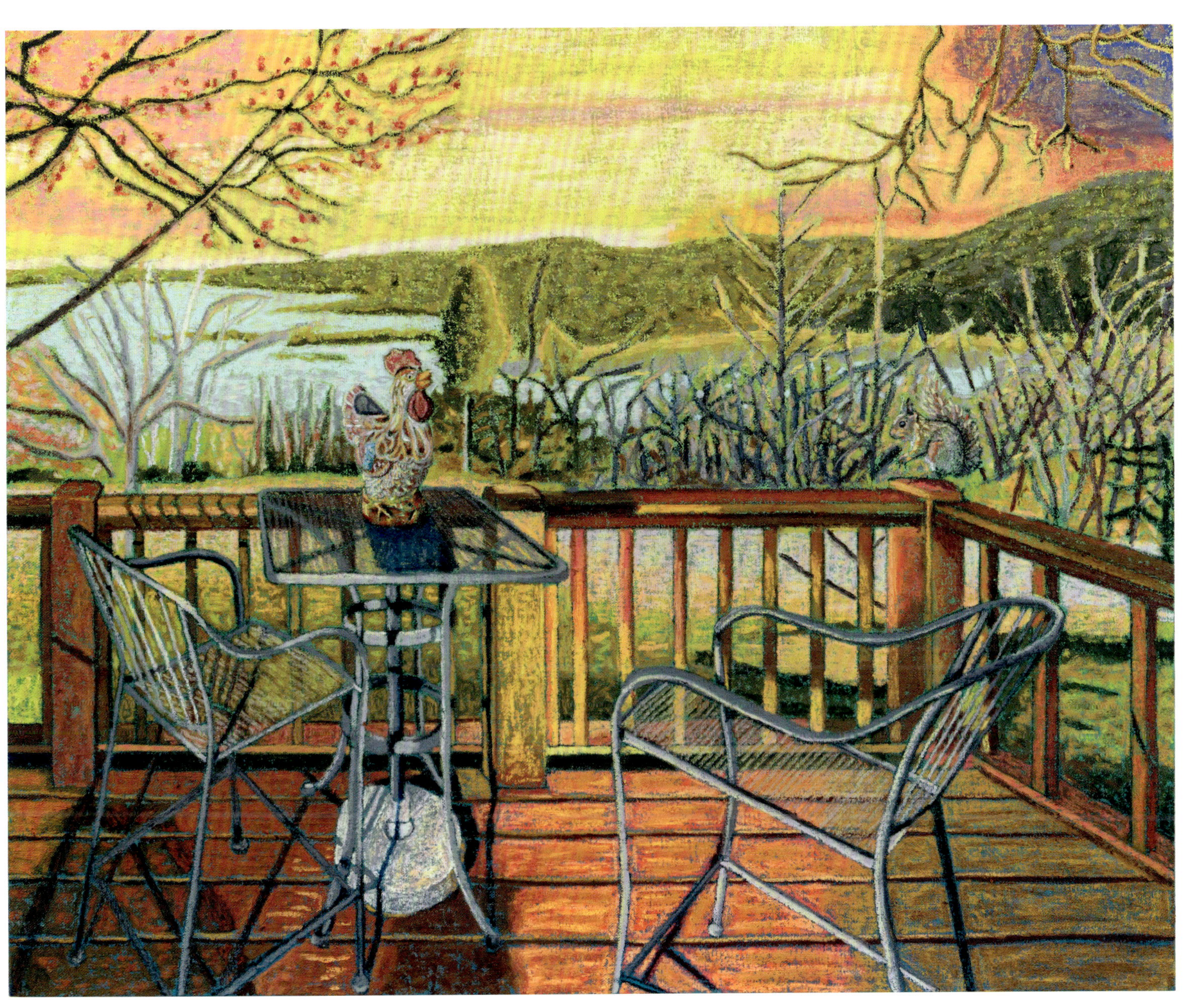

Massachusetts Porch Sitting with Squirrel & Rooster Vase, 2023, oil stick, oil pastel, and Flashe on burlap over canvas, 72 x 90 inches

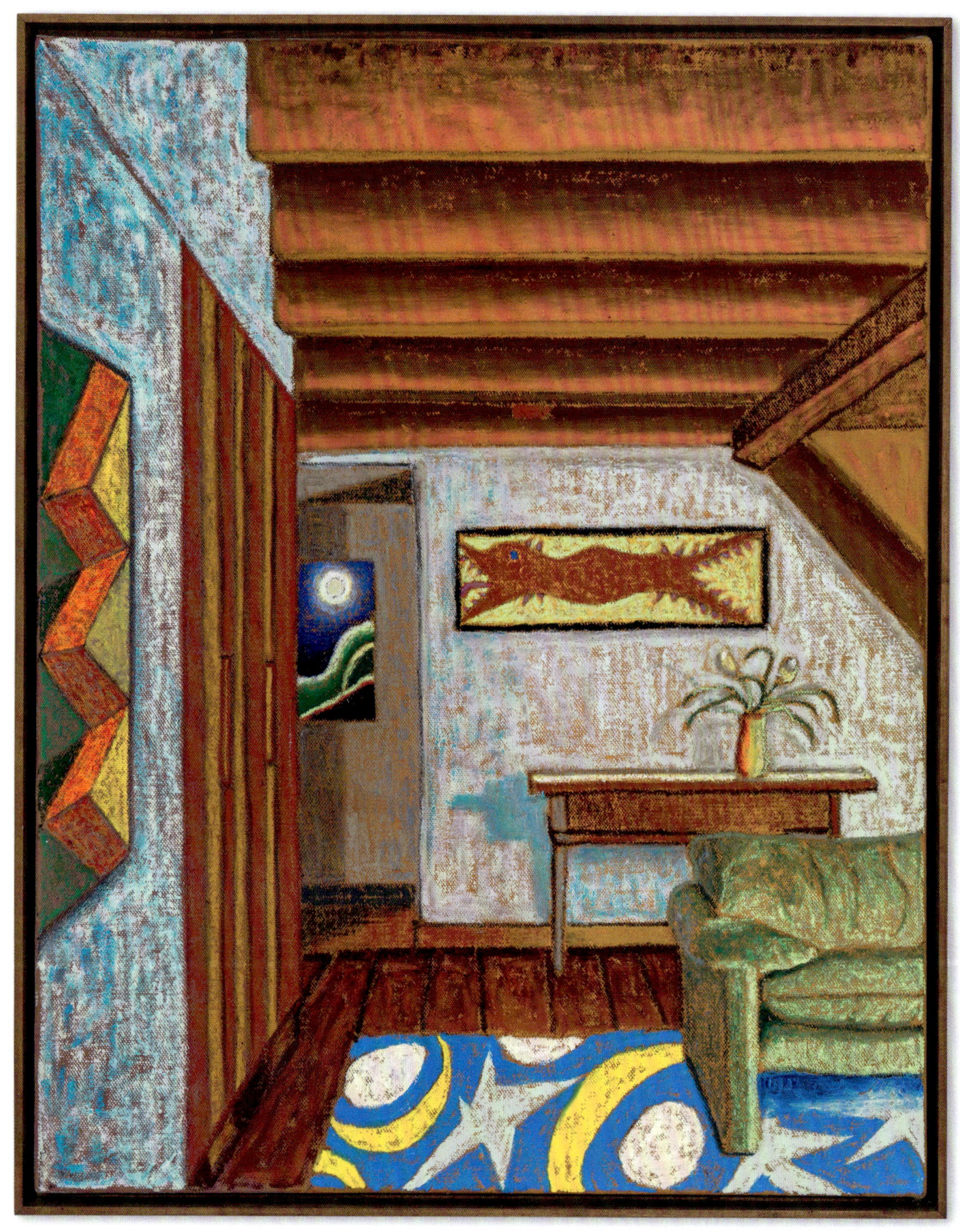

Interior with Mose Tolliver, 2021, oil stick, oil pastel, and Flashe on linen, 30 x 24 inches

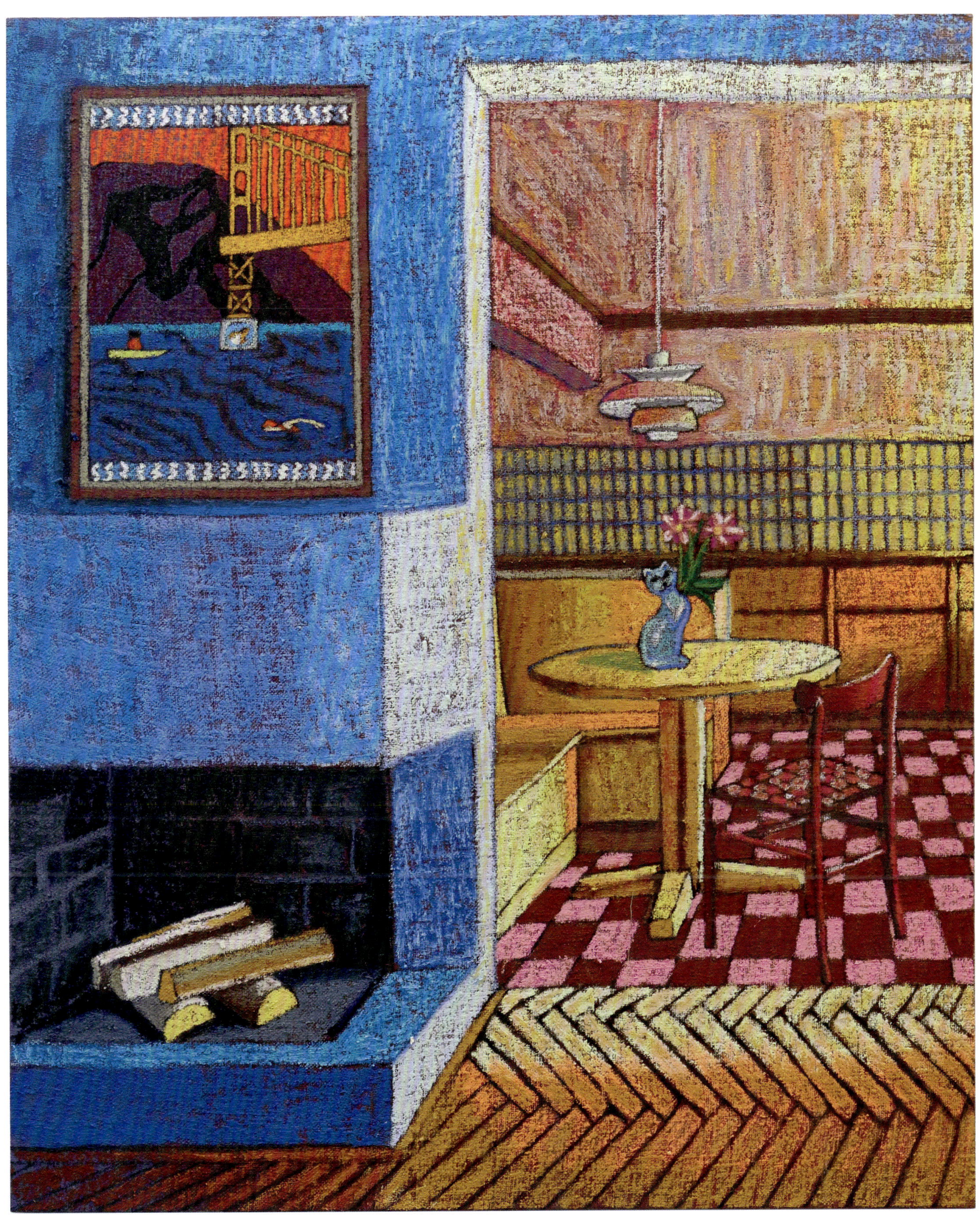

Interior with Joan Brown and Porcelain Cat Vase, 2022, oil stick, oil pastel, and Flashe on burlap over canvas, 60 x 50 inches

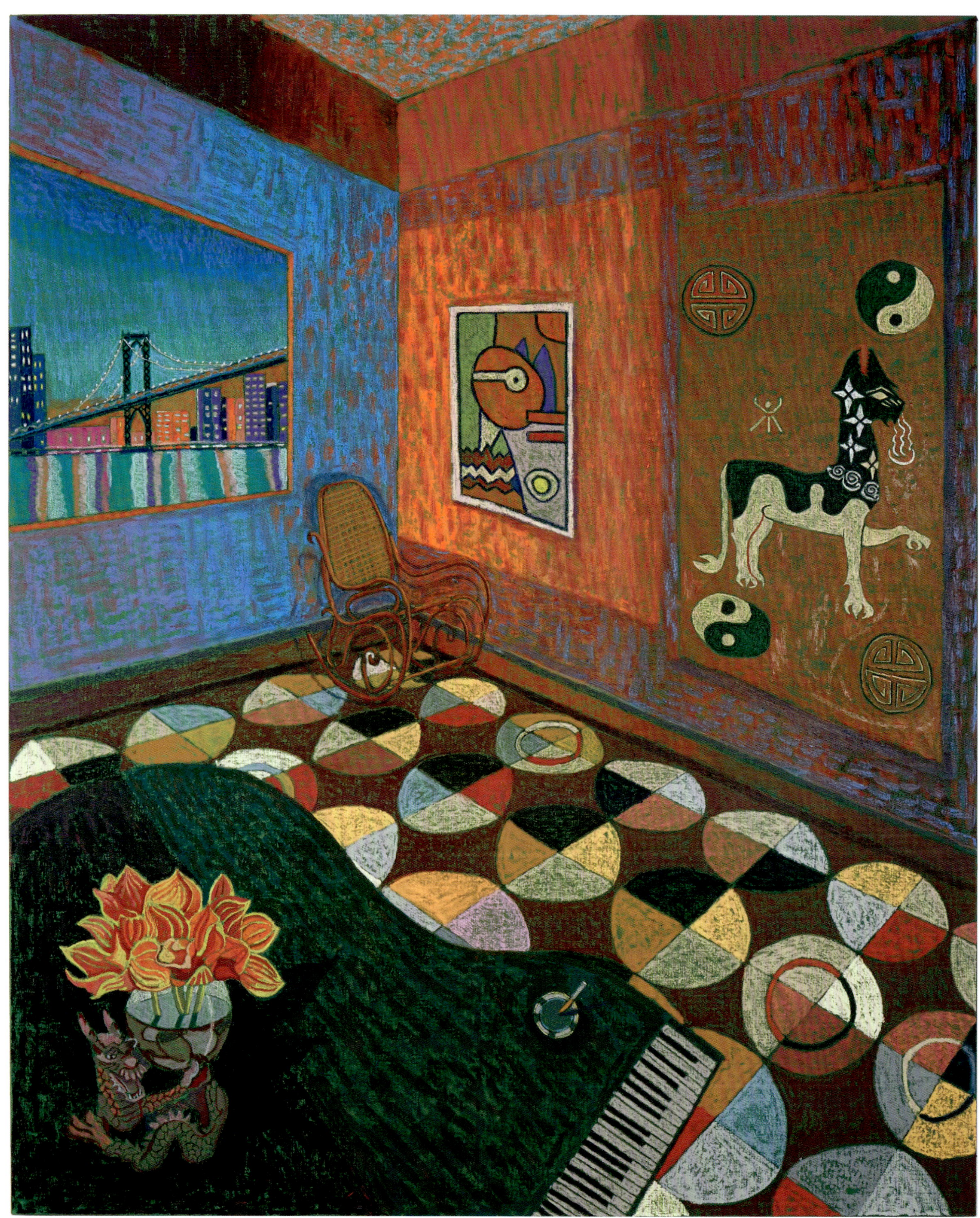

Blood Moon, 2023, oil stick, oil pastel, and Flashe on linen, 84 x 72 inches

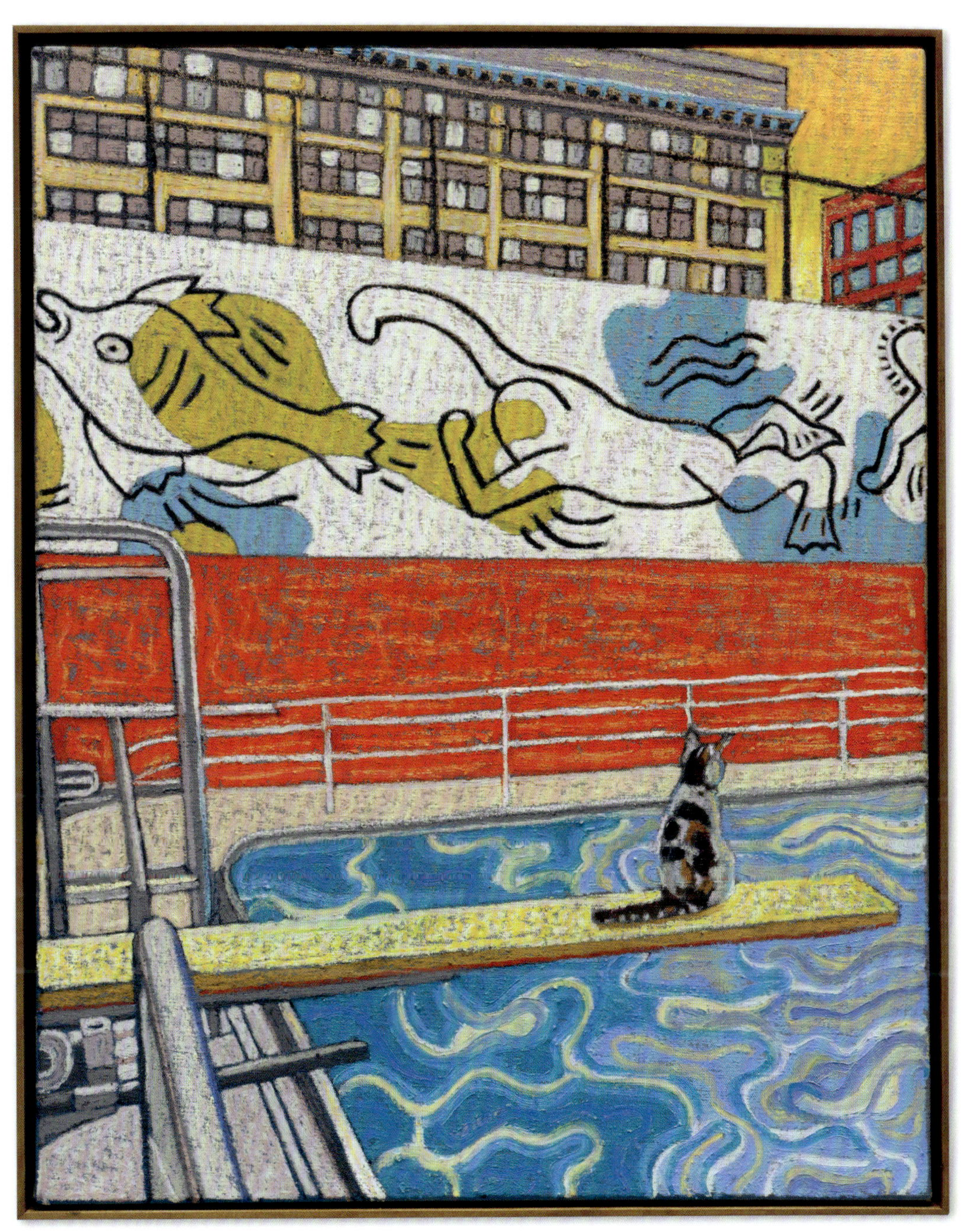

Carmine St. (Keith Haring Pool), 2023, oil stick, oil pastel, and Flashe on linen, 30 x 24 inches

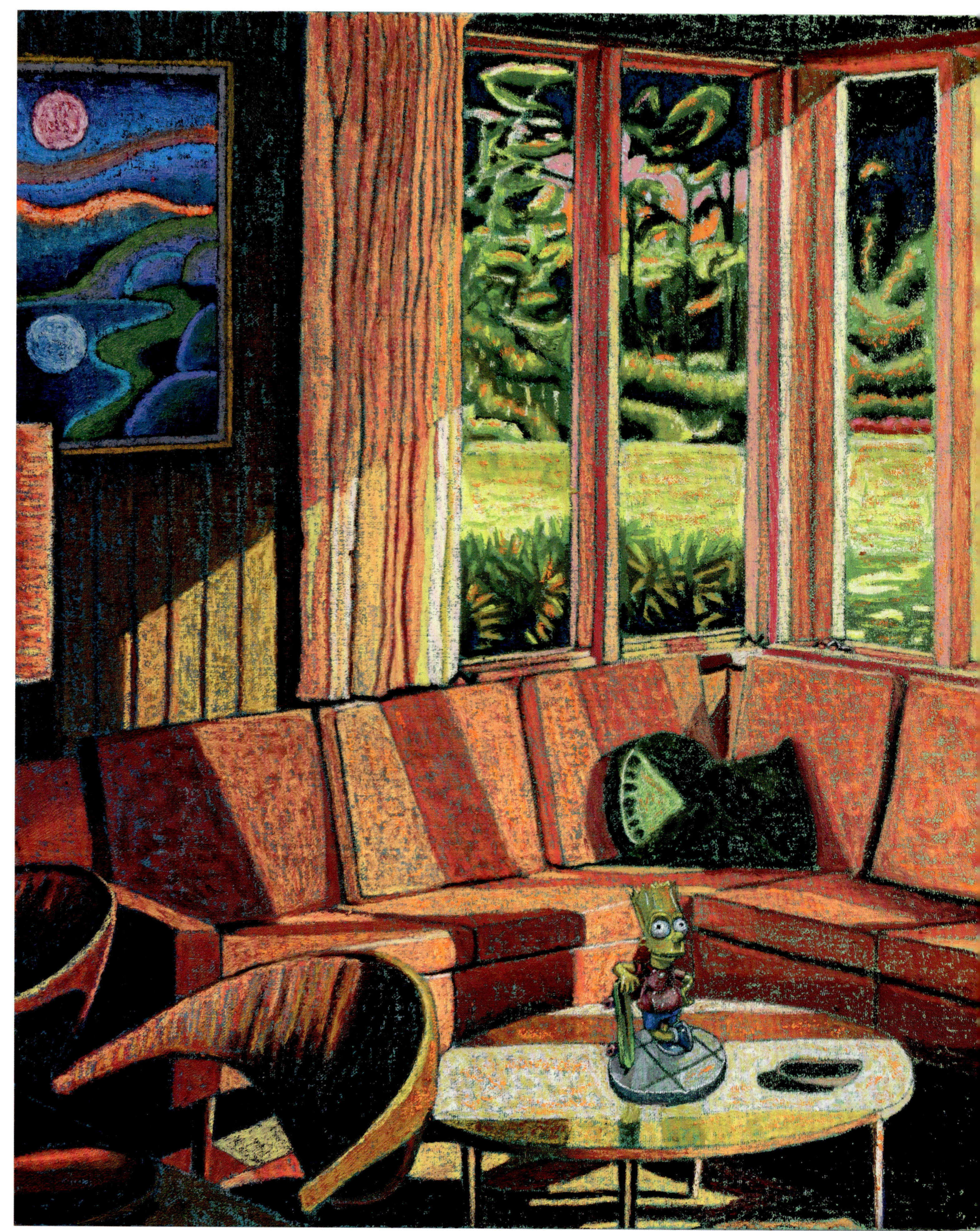

Suburban Sunset with Bart Simpson, 2023, oil stick, oil pastel, and Flashe on burlap over canv

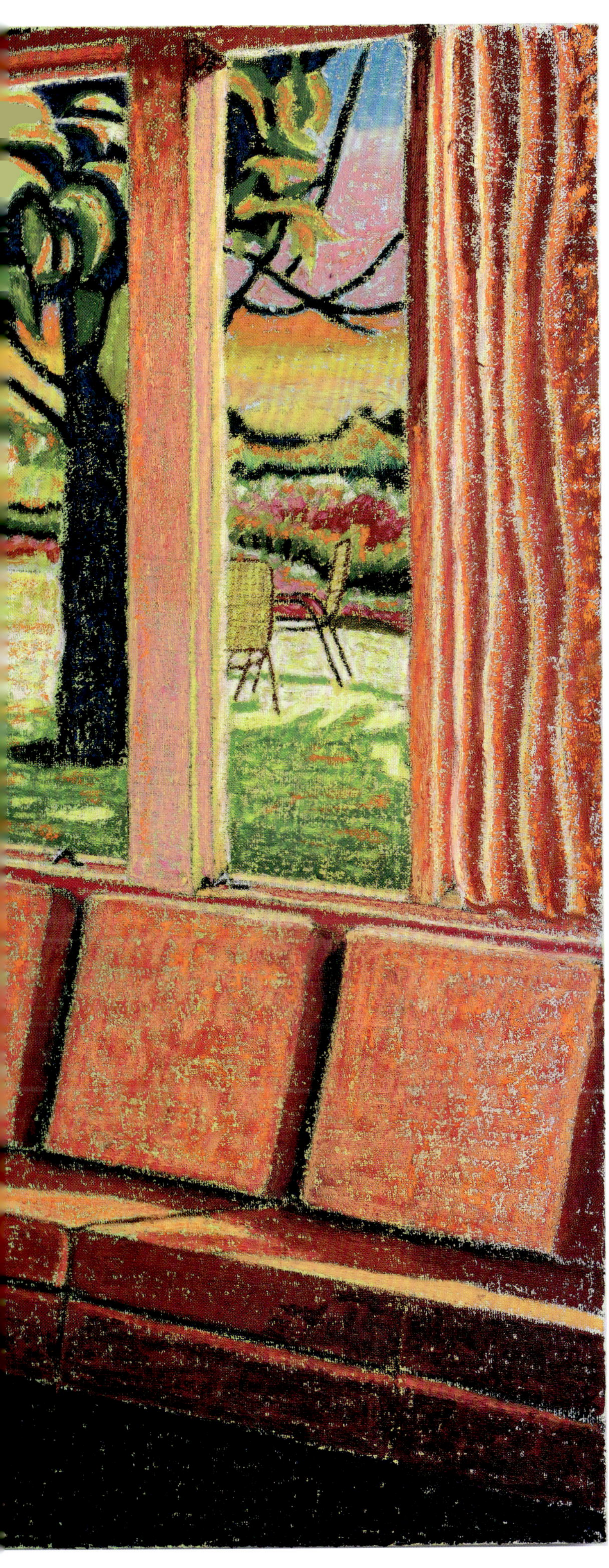

x 90 inches

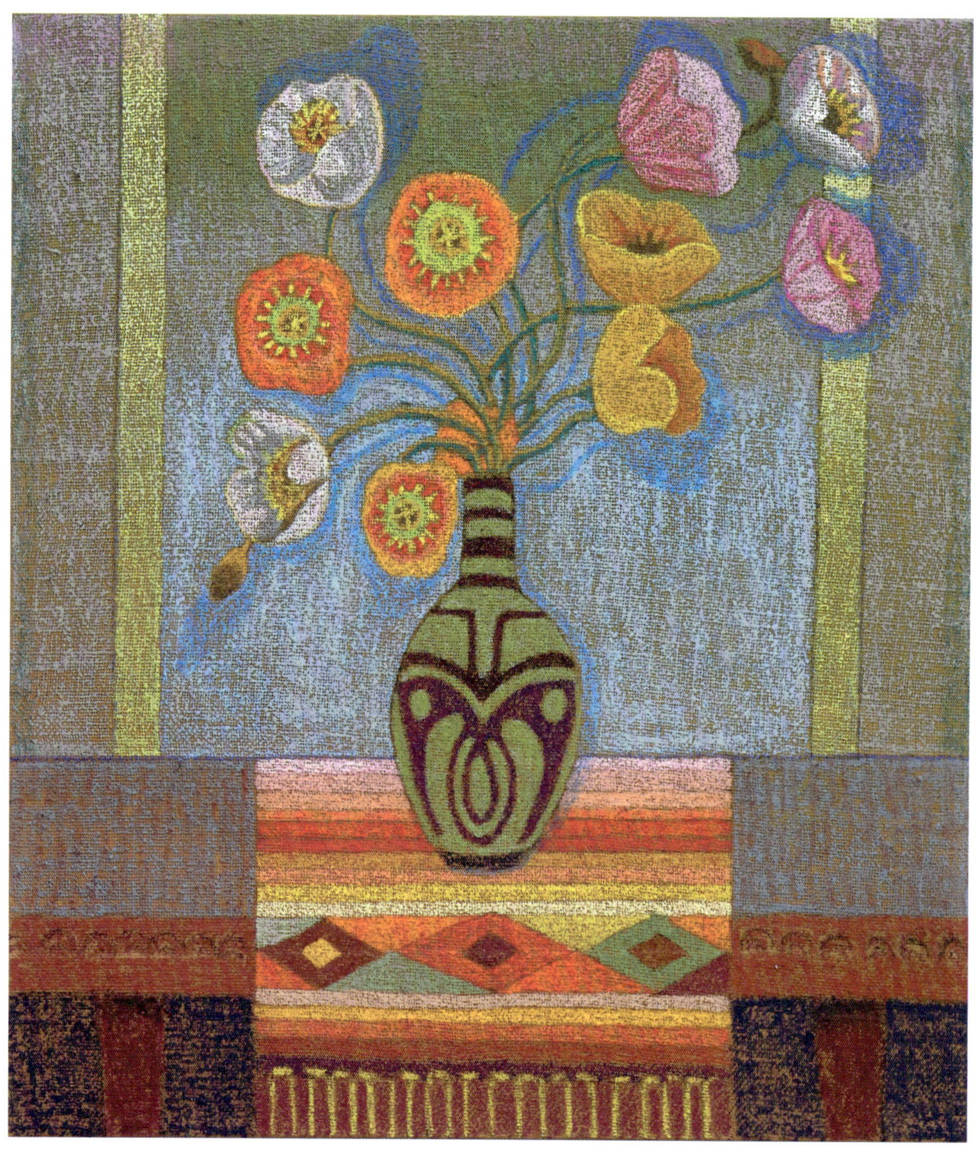

Peruvian Still Life in Gowanus, 2020, oil stick, oil pastel and Flashe on burlap over canvas, 36 x 32 inches

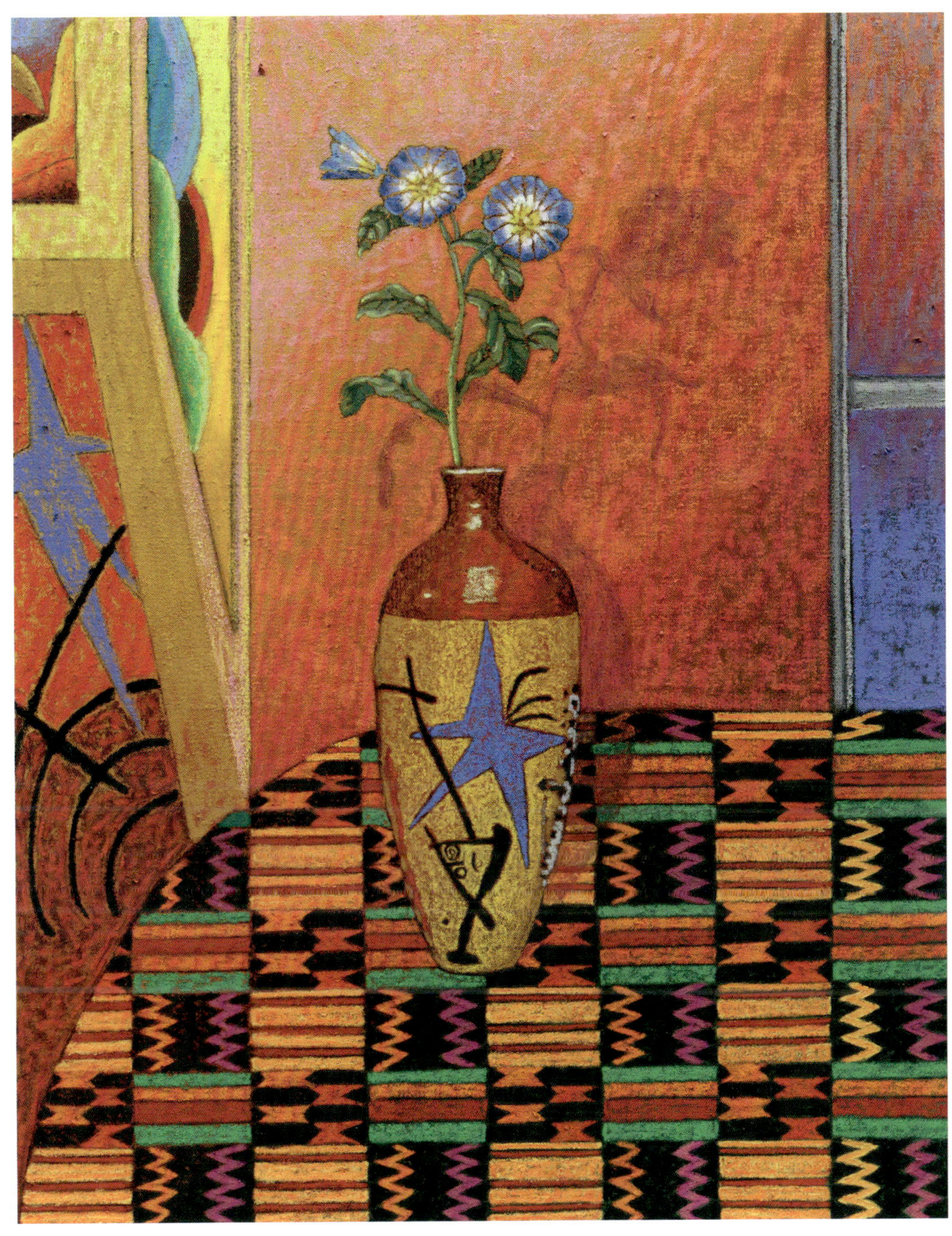

Still Life With Miró Vase & African Fabric, 2023, oil stick, oil pastel, and Flashe on linen, 45 x 36 inches

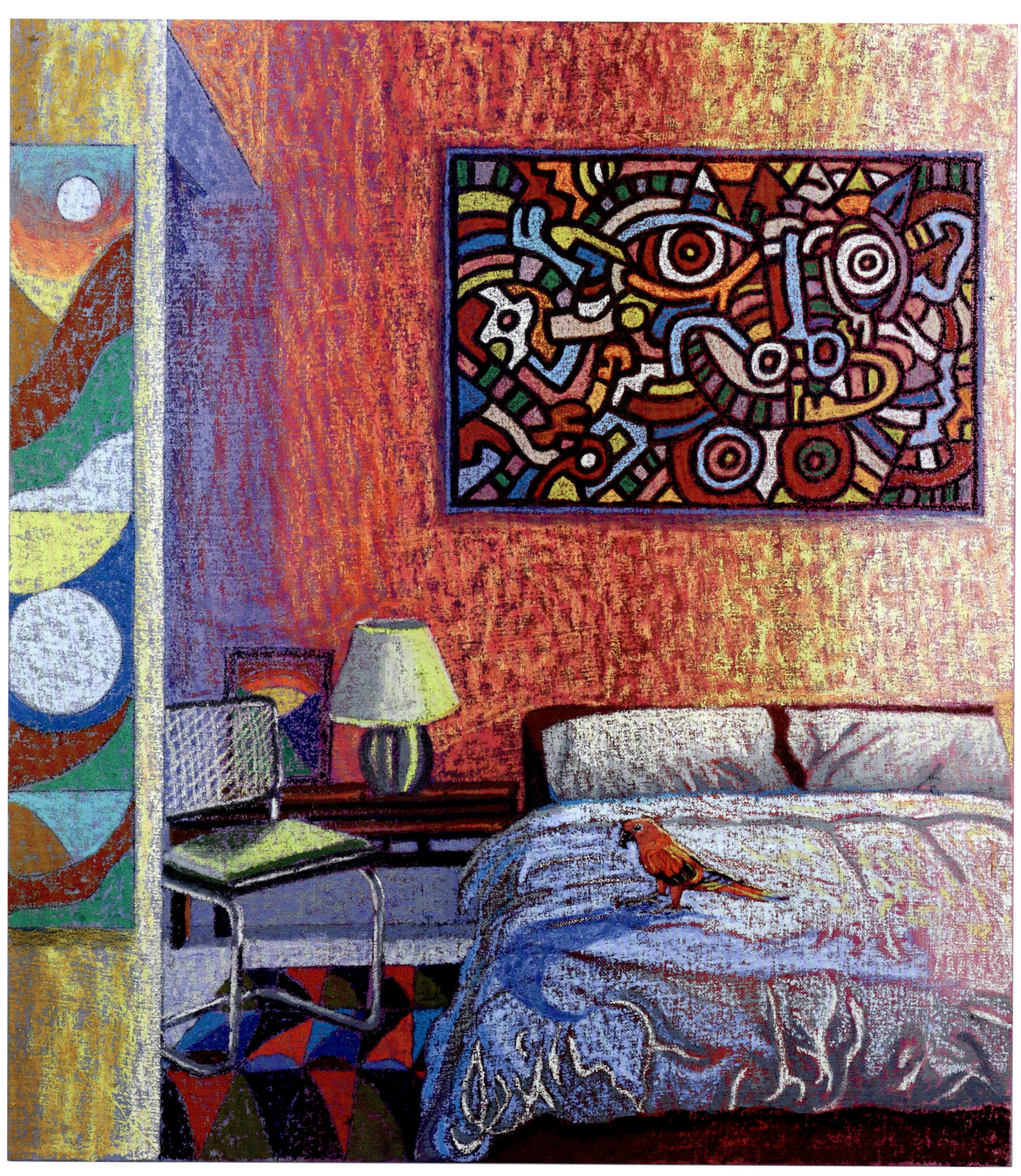

Interior with Keith Haring & Parrot, 2022, oil stick, oil pastel, and Flashe on burlap over canvas, 66 3/8 x 60 inches

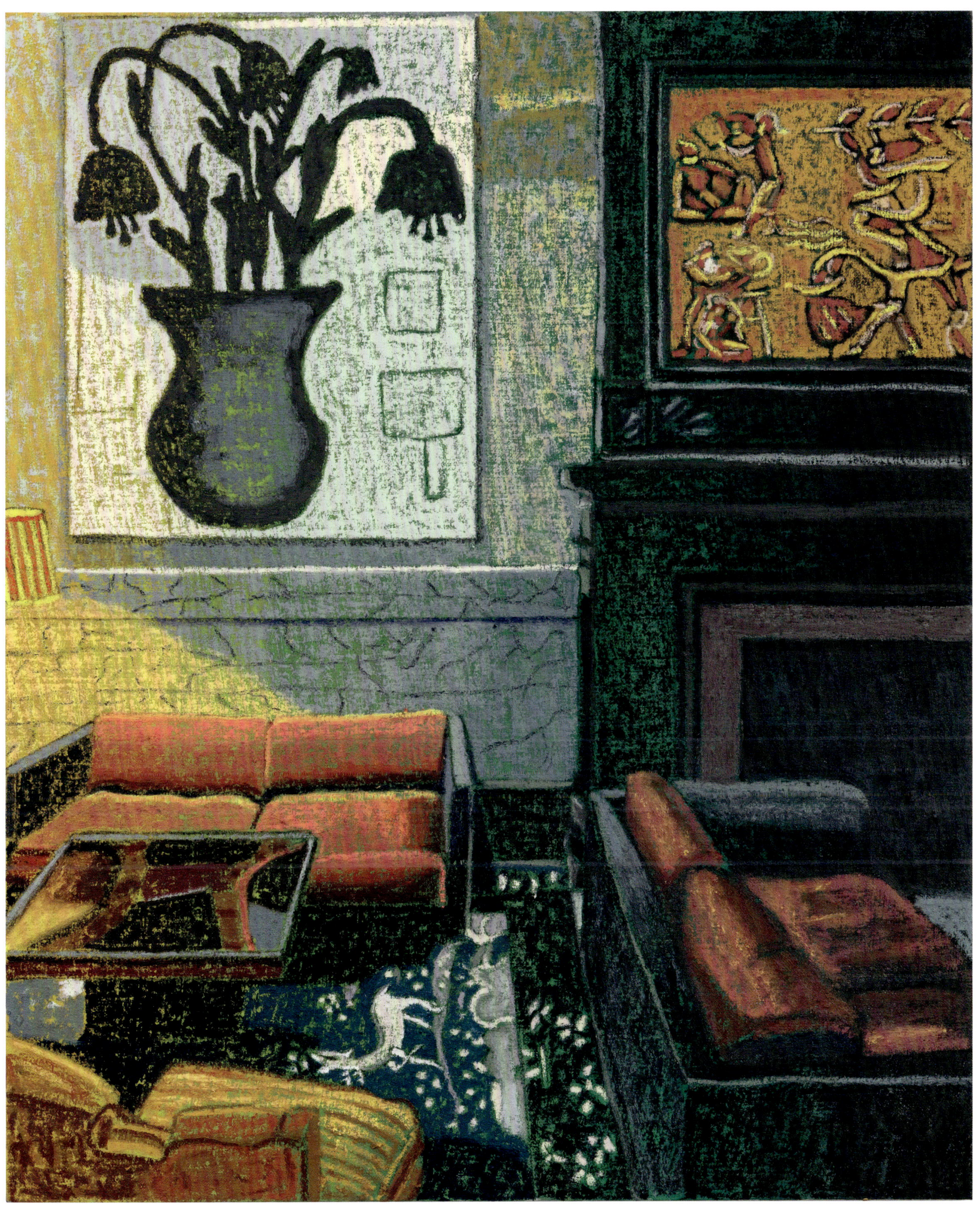

Midnight at the Chelsea Hotel, 2022, oil stick, oil pastel, and Flashe on burlap over canvas, 72 x 60 inches

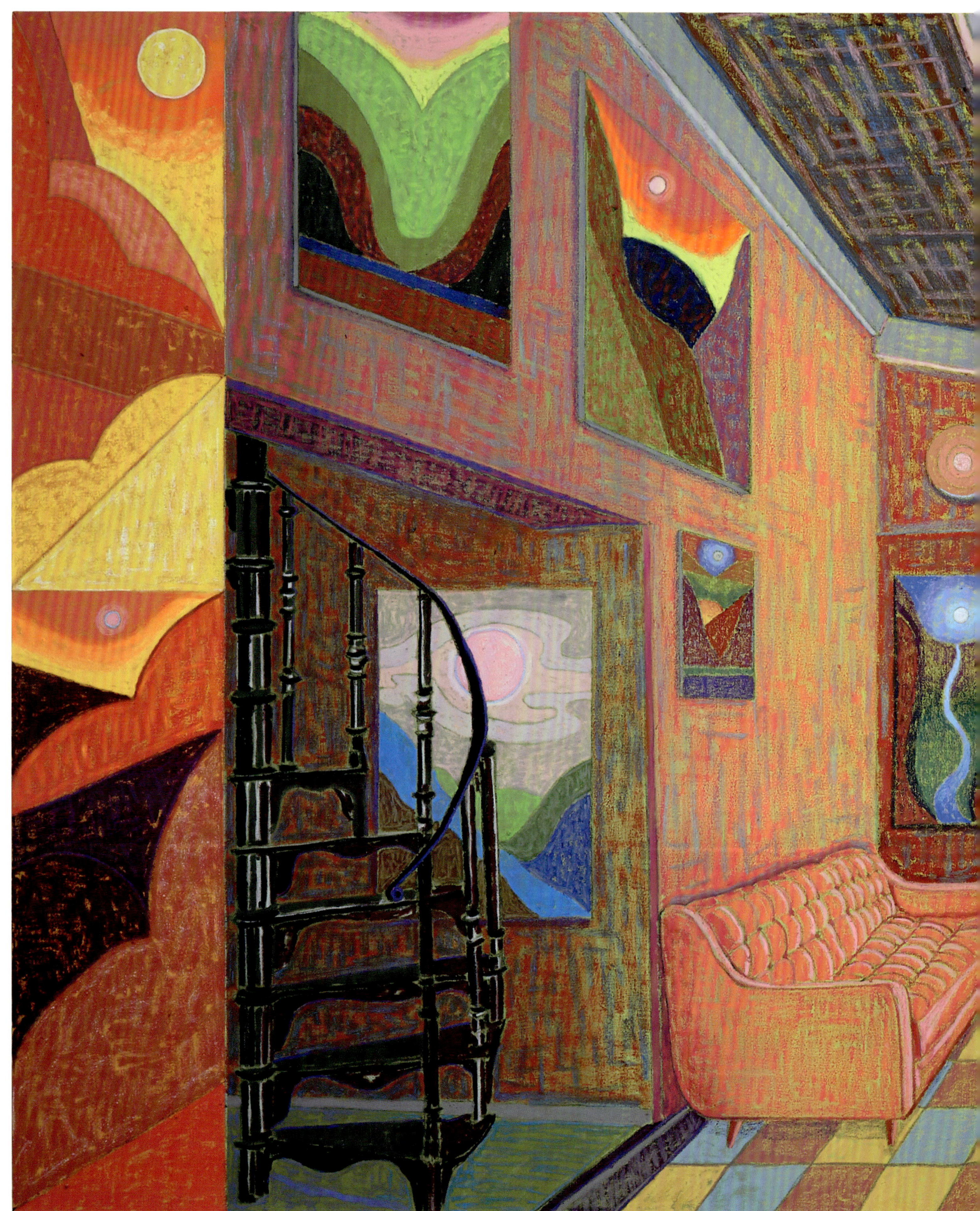

Moon & Sun Salon (The Cycle of the Day), 2021,

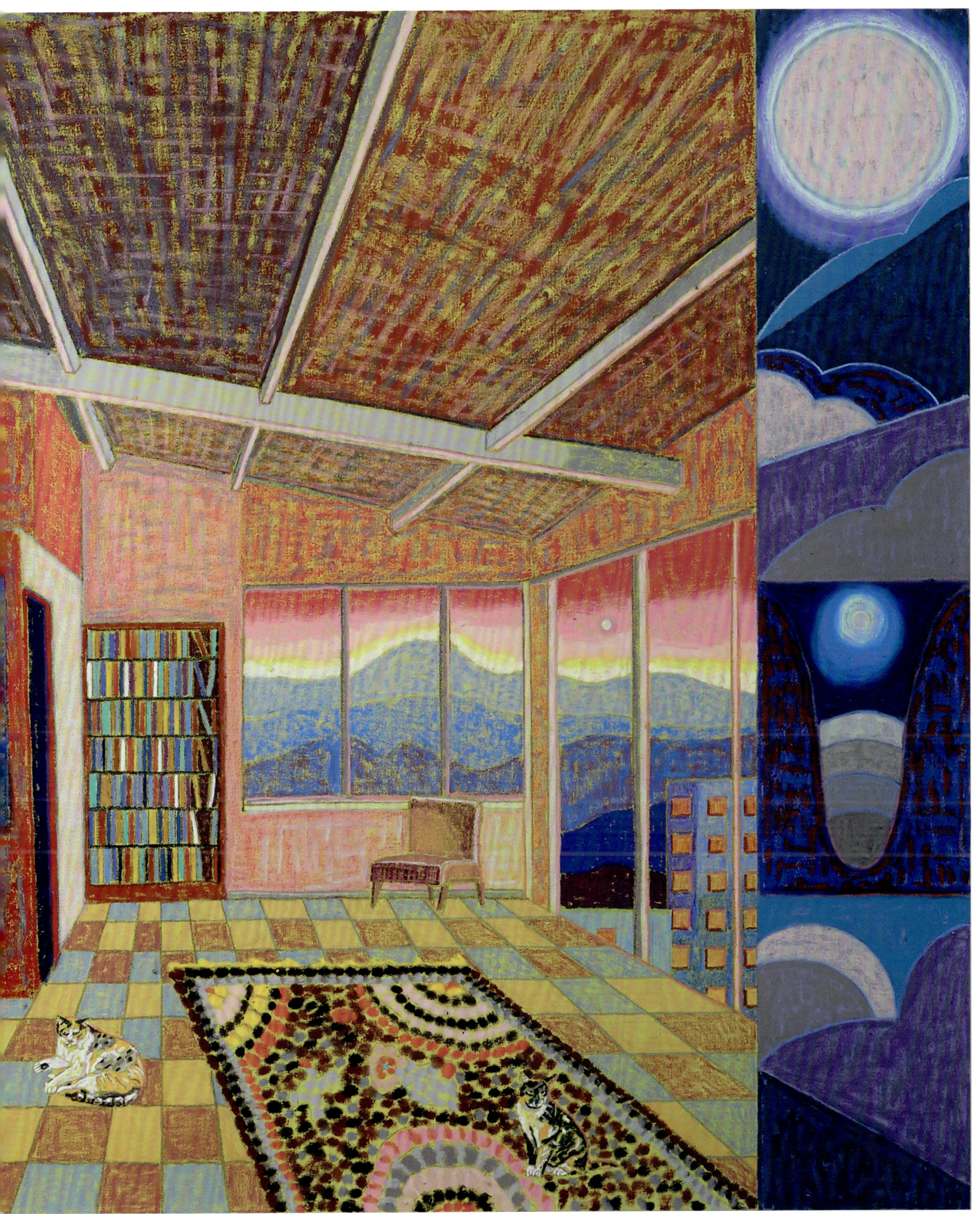

ck, oil pastel, and Flashe on linen, 78 ½ x 134 inches

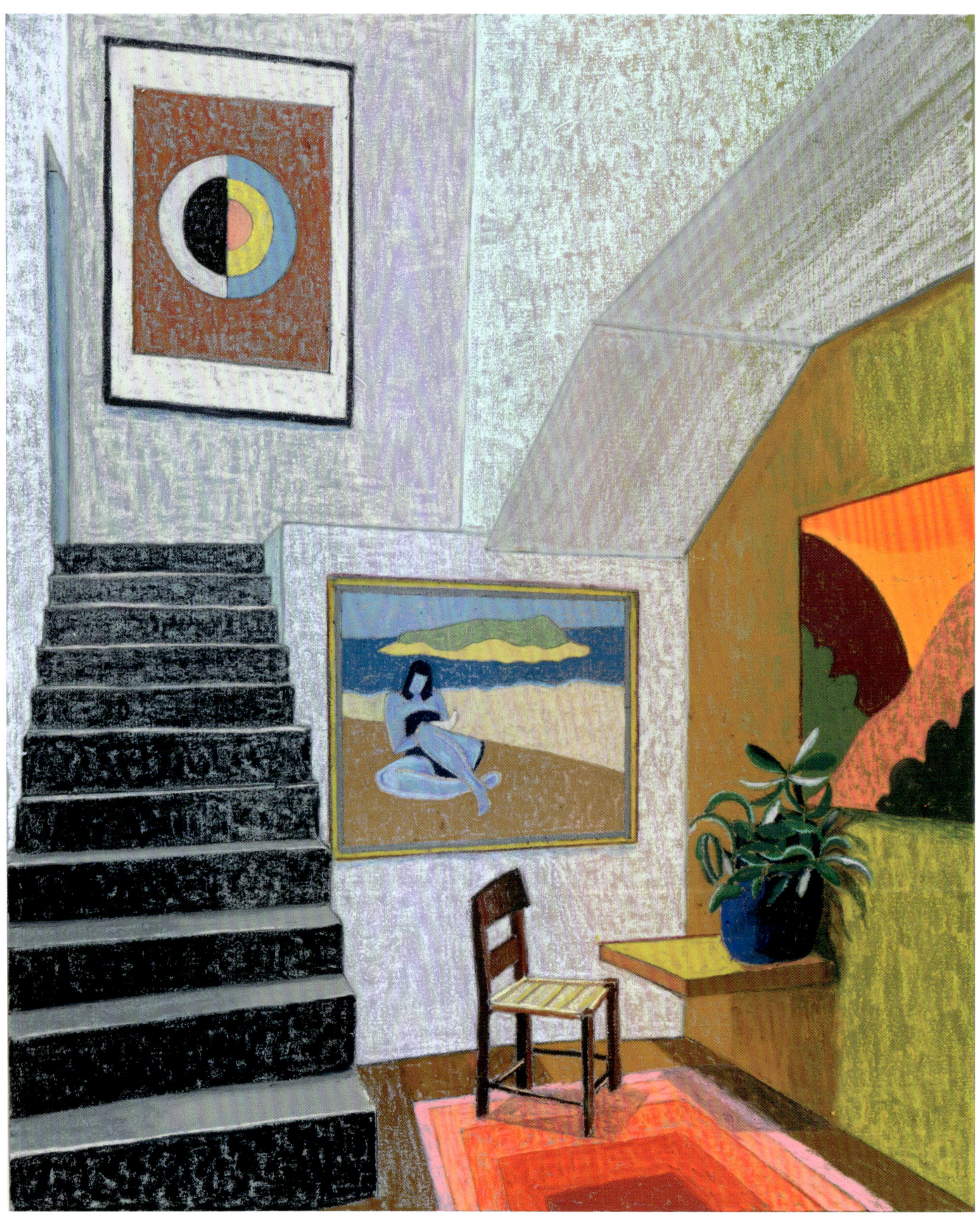

Luis Barragan–Inspired Interior with Hilma af Klint & Milton Avery, 2021, oil stick, oil pastel, and Flashe on linen, 60 x 50 inches

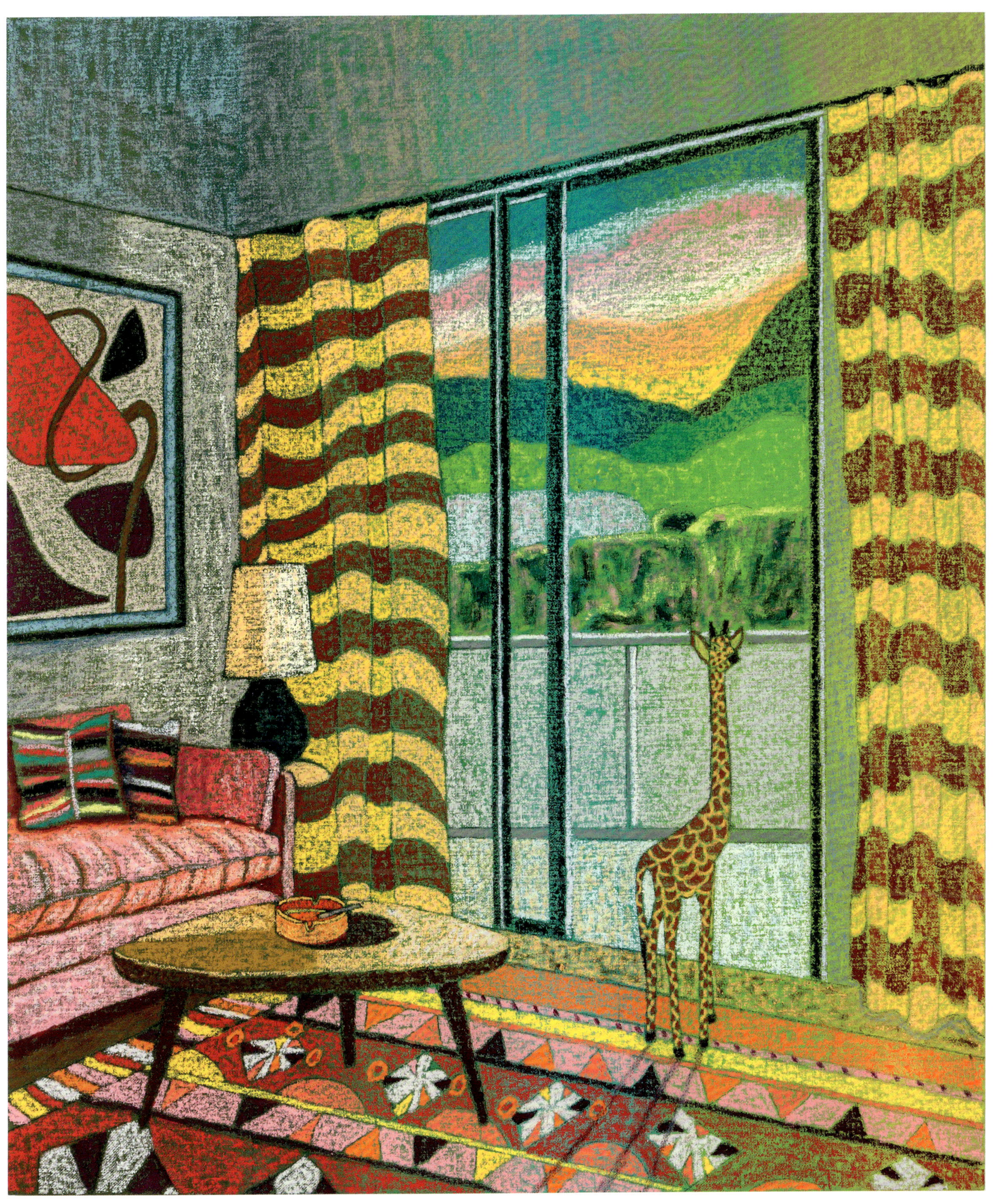

Interior with Giraffe Sculpture & Calder Print, 2021, oil stick, oil pastel, and Flashe on burlap, 84 x 72 inches

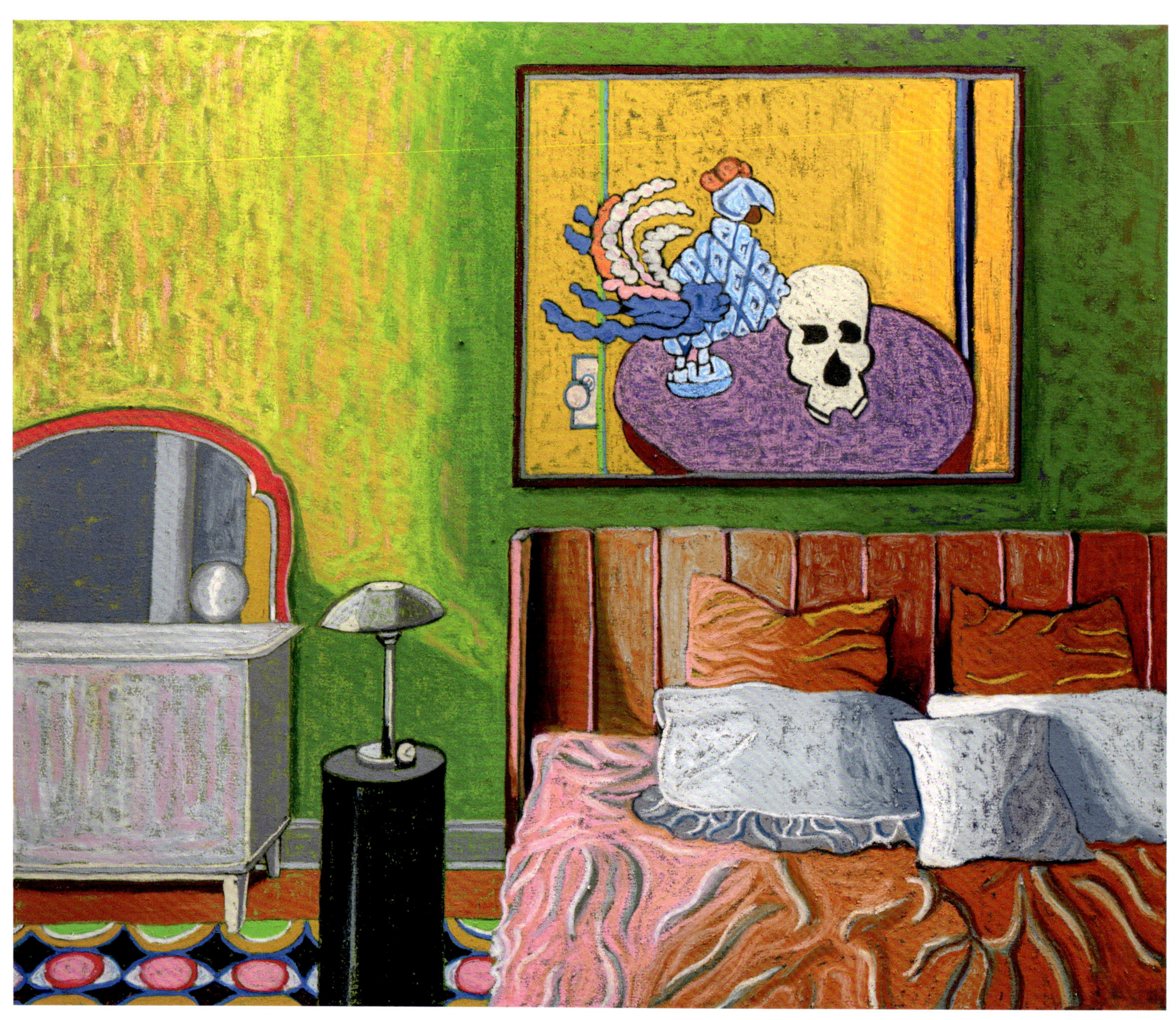

Bedroom Interior with Still Life with Skull, 2022, oil stick, oil pastel, and Flashe on burlap over canvas, 60 x 72 inches

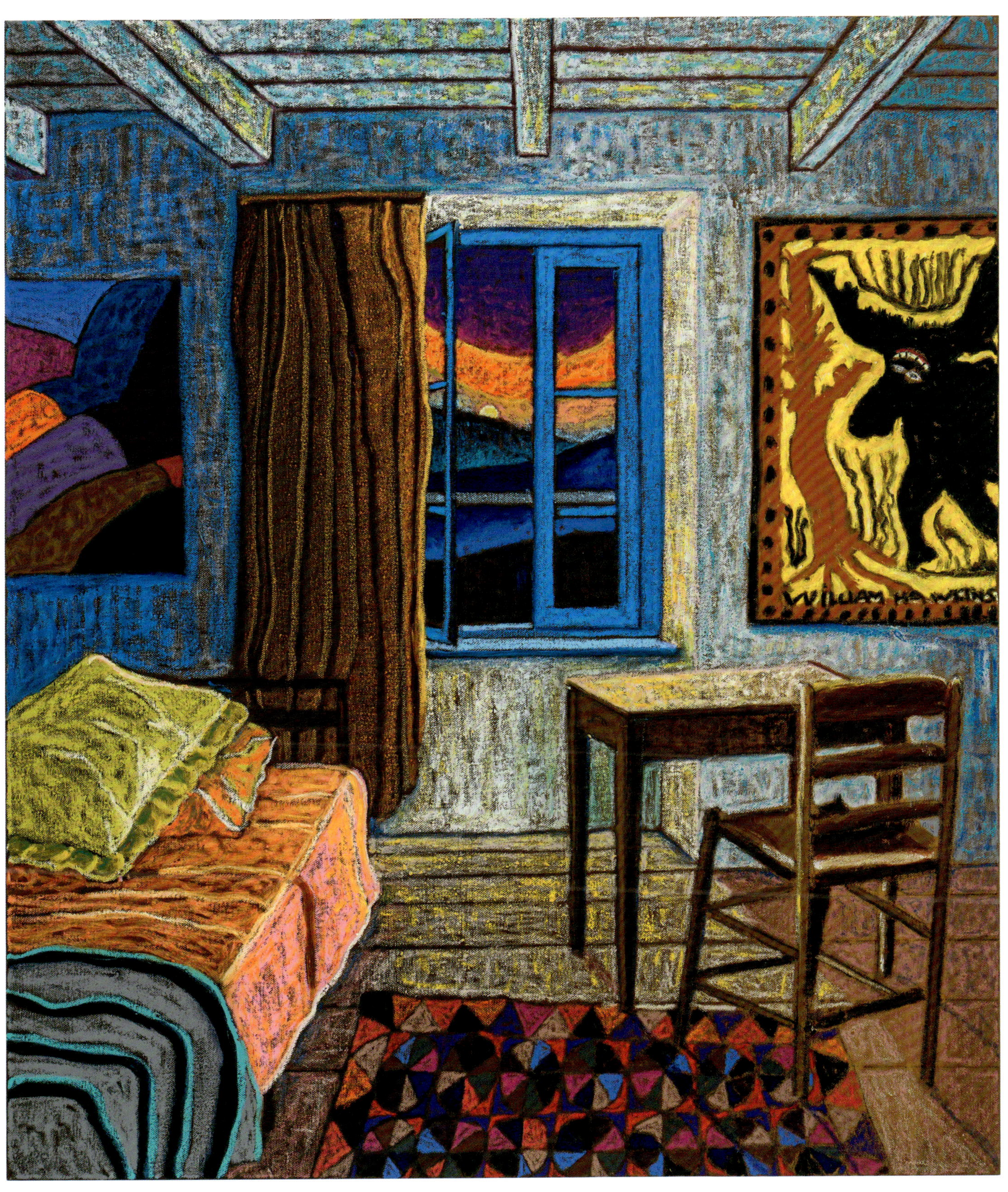

Sunrise with William Hawkins, 2021, oil stick, oil pastel, and Flashe on linen, 46 x 41 inches

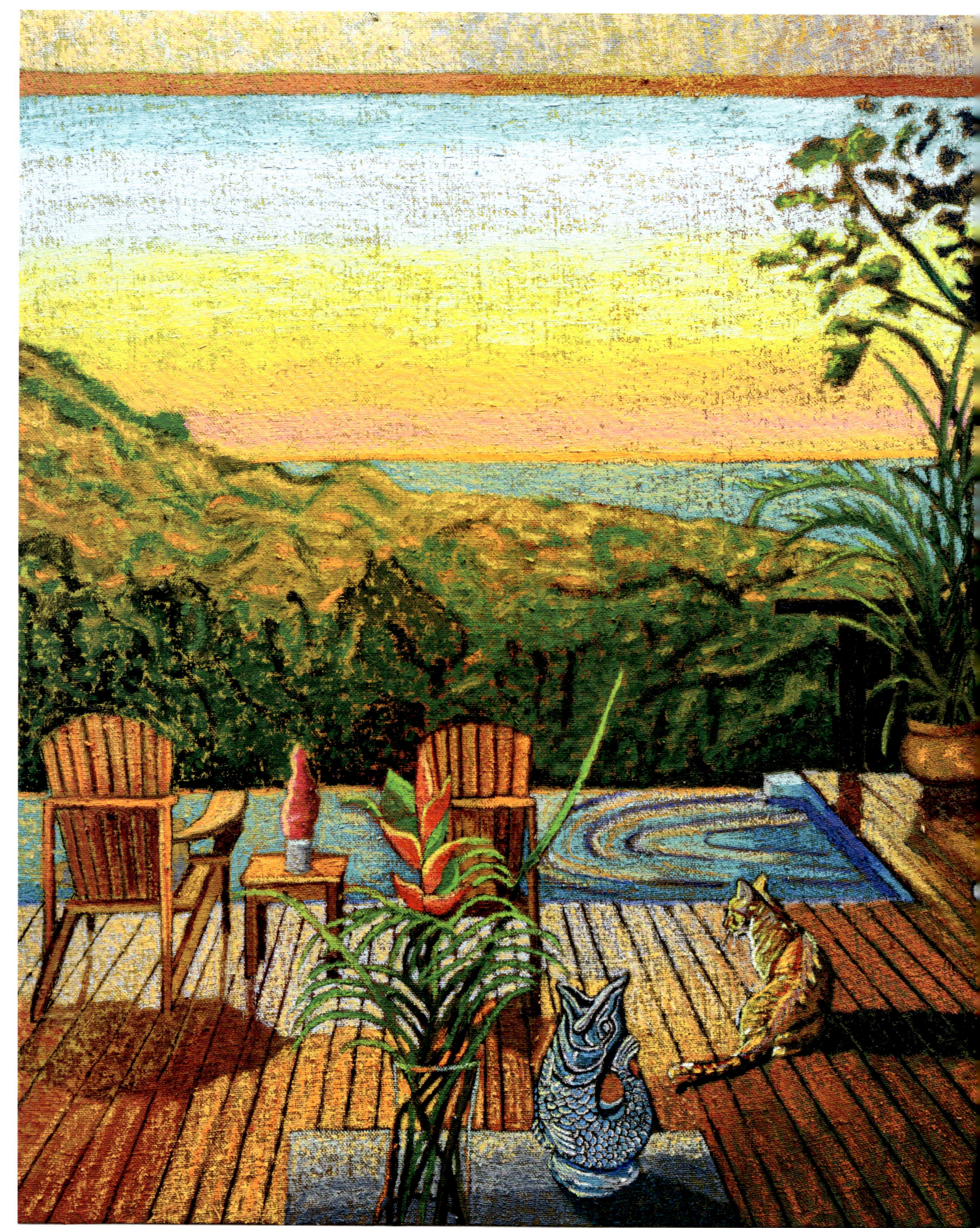

Wanderlust Painting, 2023, oil stick, oil pastel, and Flashe on burlap over canvas, 68 x

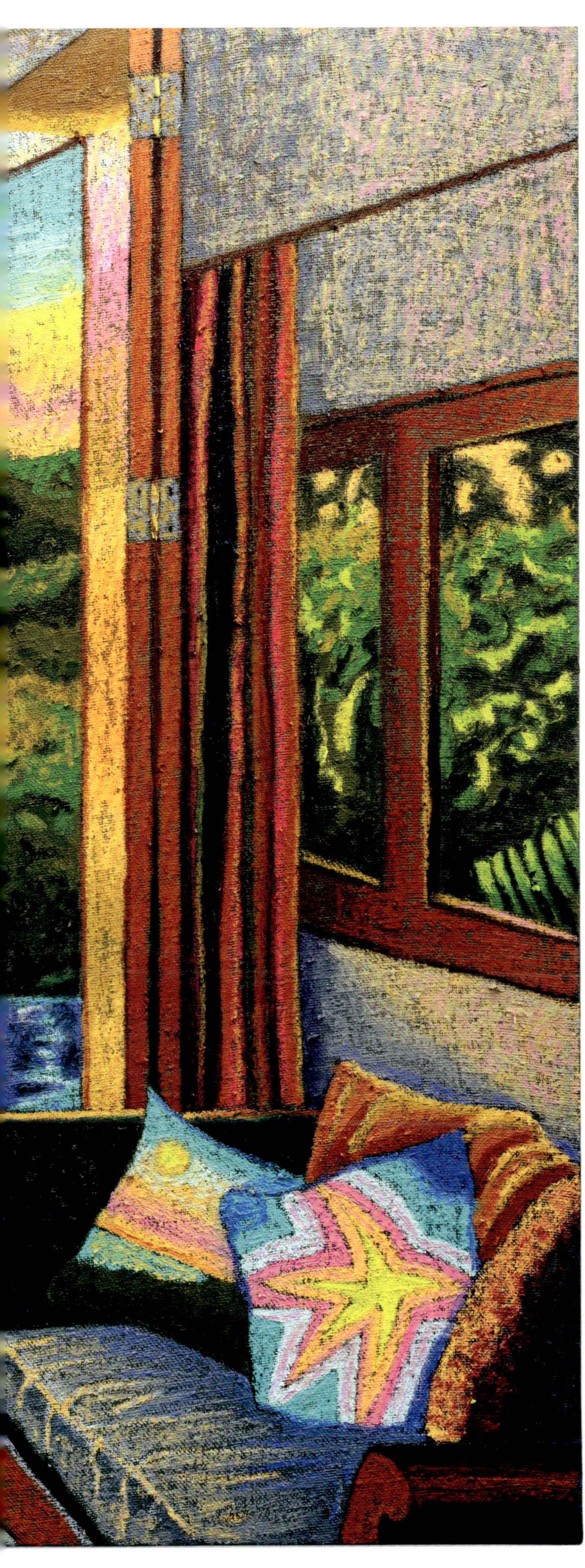

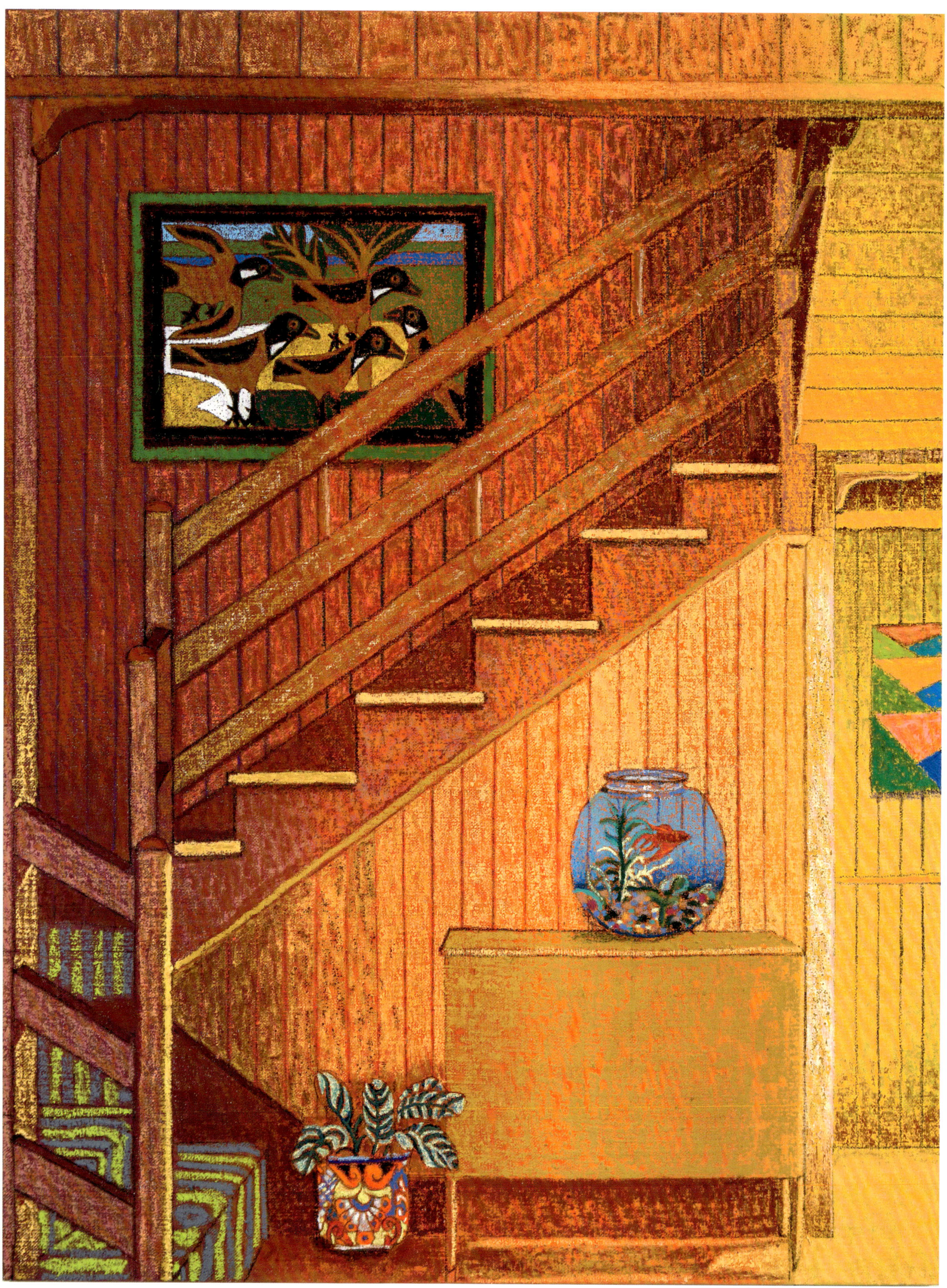

Interior with Eddie Arning, Beta Fish, & Mexican Vase, 2021, oil stick, oil pastel and Flashe on burlap over canvas, 78 x 60 inches

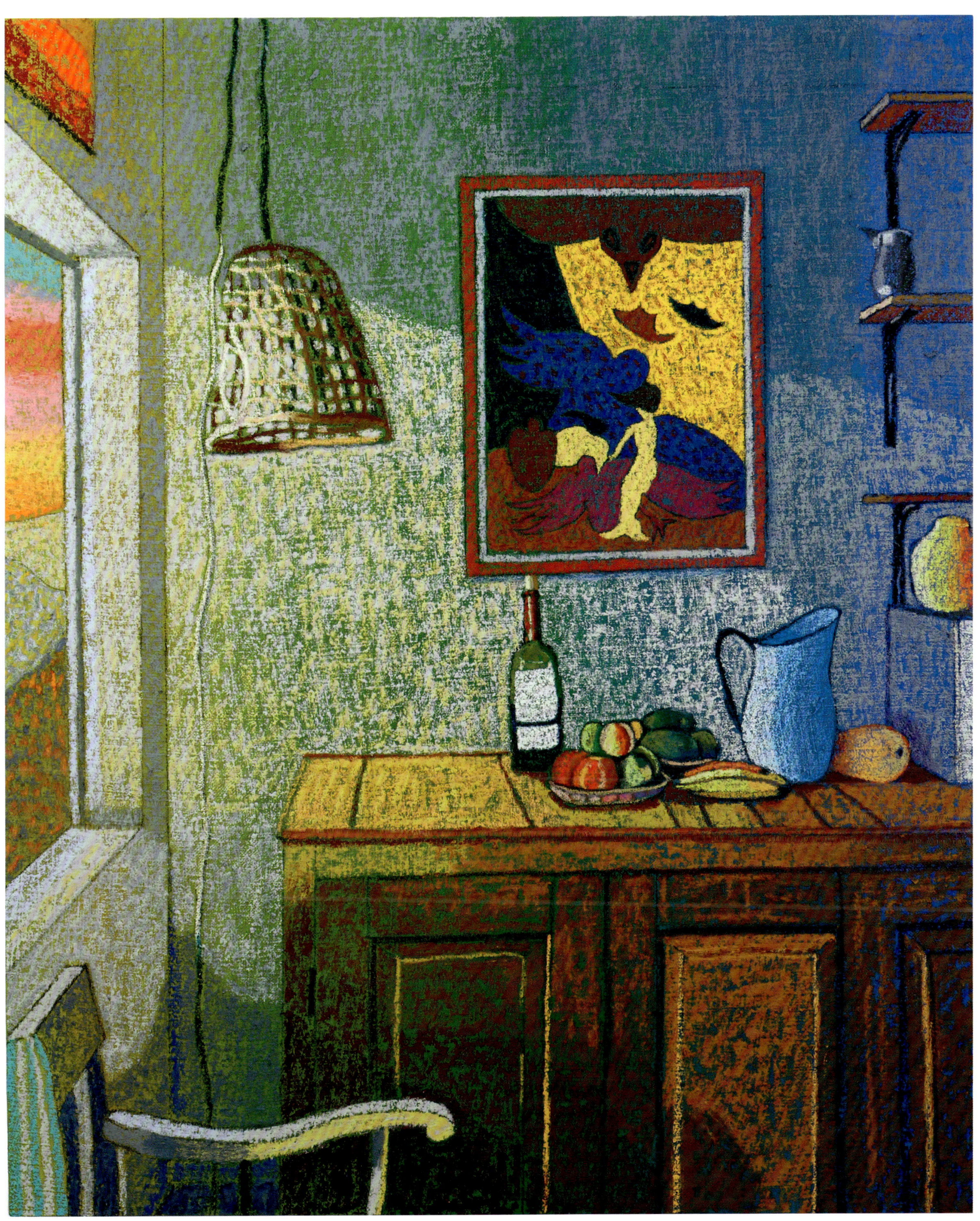

Interior with Bob Thompson, 2022, oil stick, oil pastel, and Flashe on burlap over canvas, 72 x 60 inches

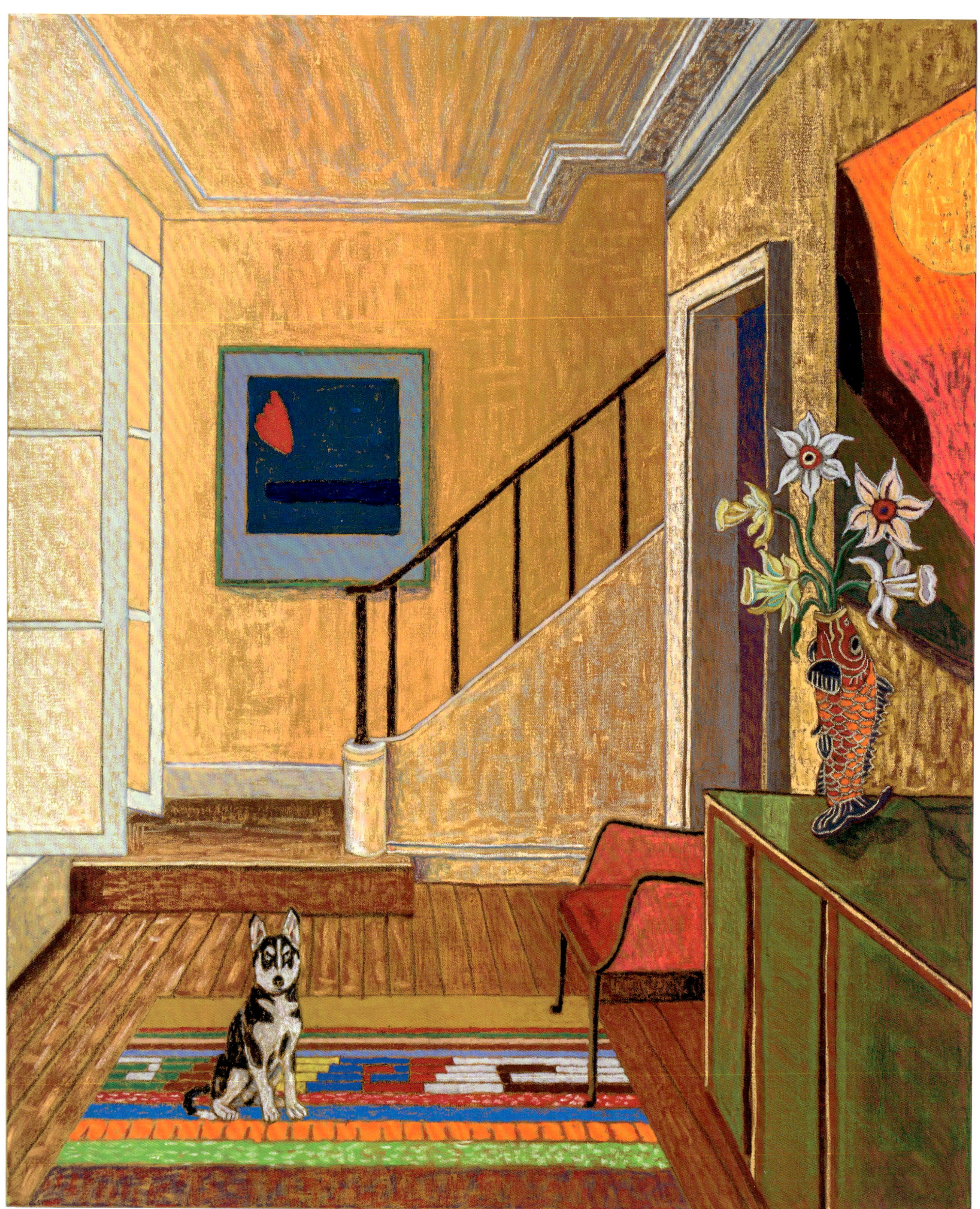

Interior with Husky Pup & Forrest Bess, 2021, oil stick, oil pastel, and Flashe on linen, 60 x 50 in inches

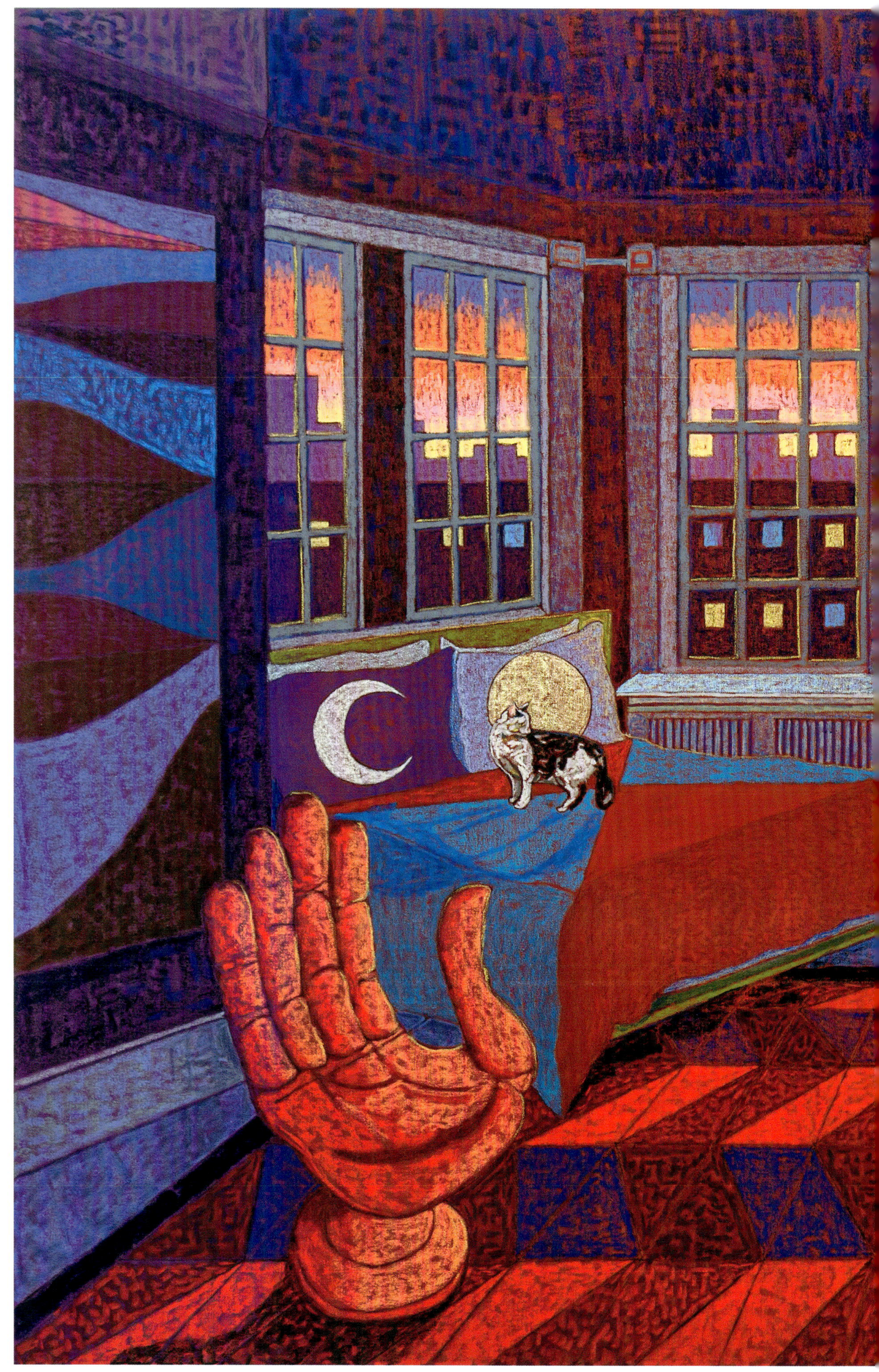

The Parrot & The Cat, 2021, oil stick,

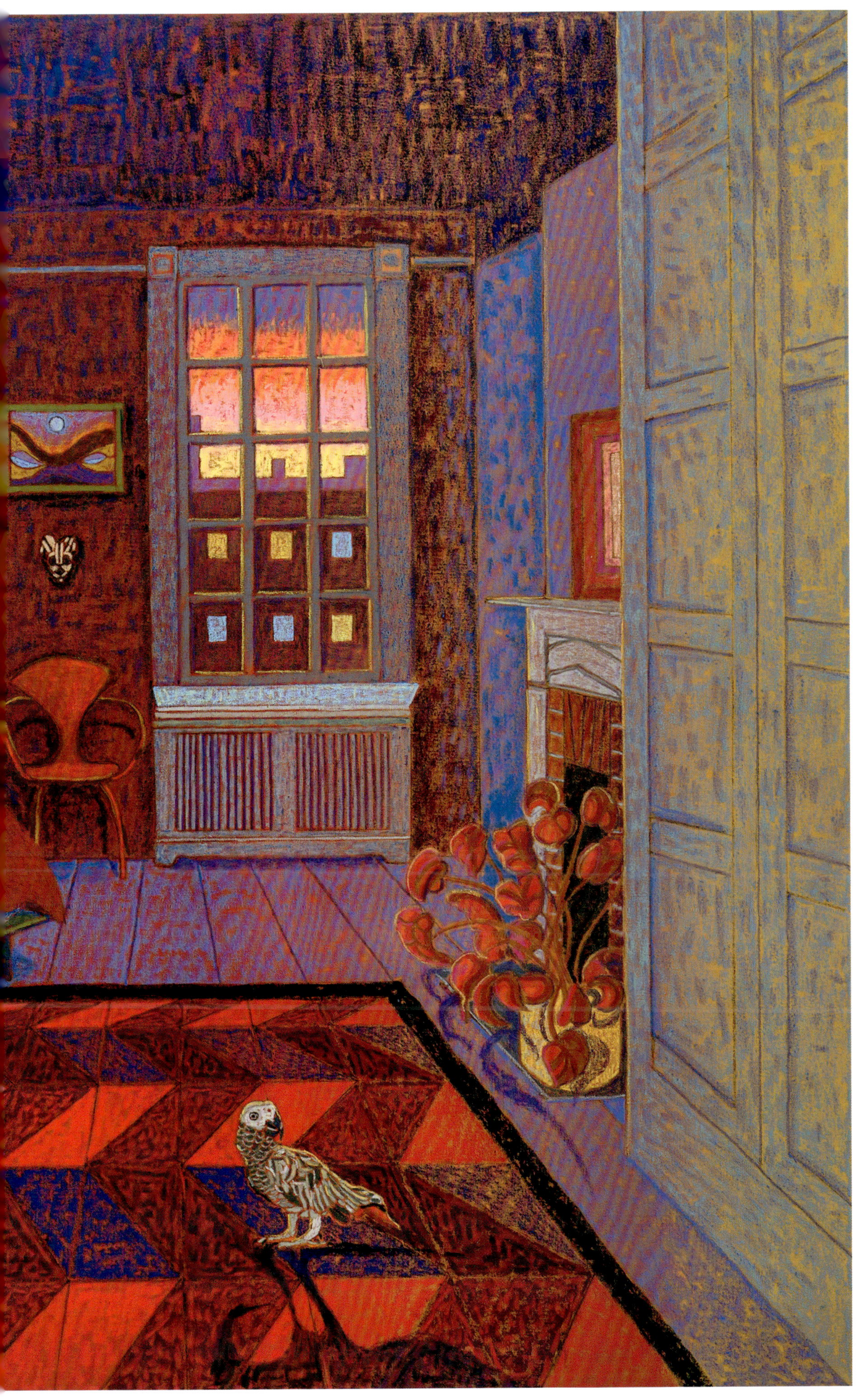

stel, and Flashe on linen, 79 x 103 inches

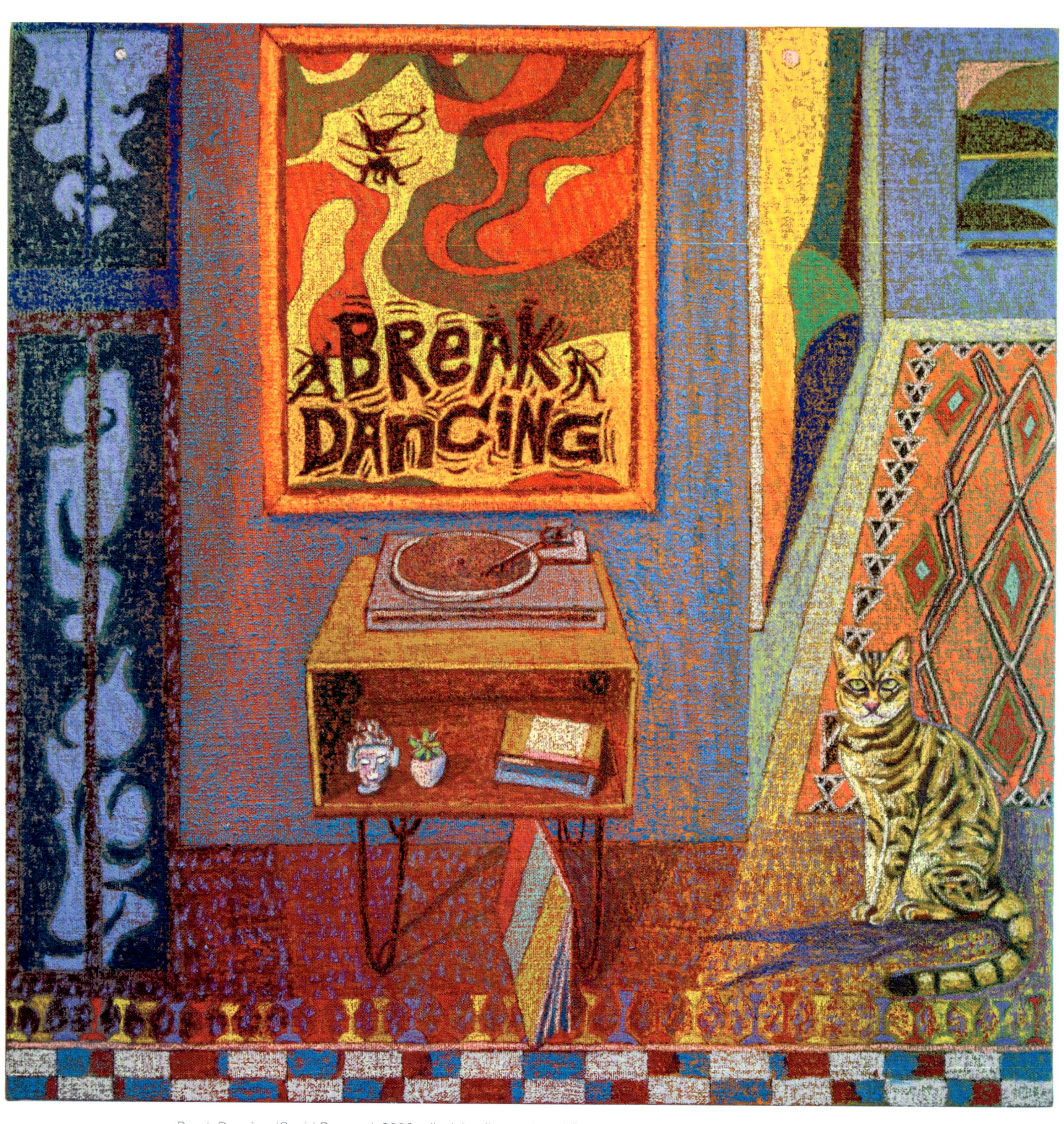

Break Dancing (Covid Dreams), 2020, oil stick, oil pastel, and Flashe on burlap over drop cloth, 54 x 54 inches

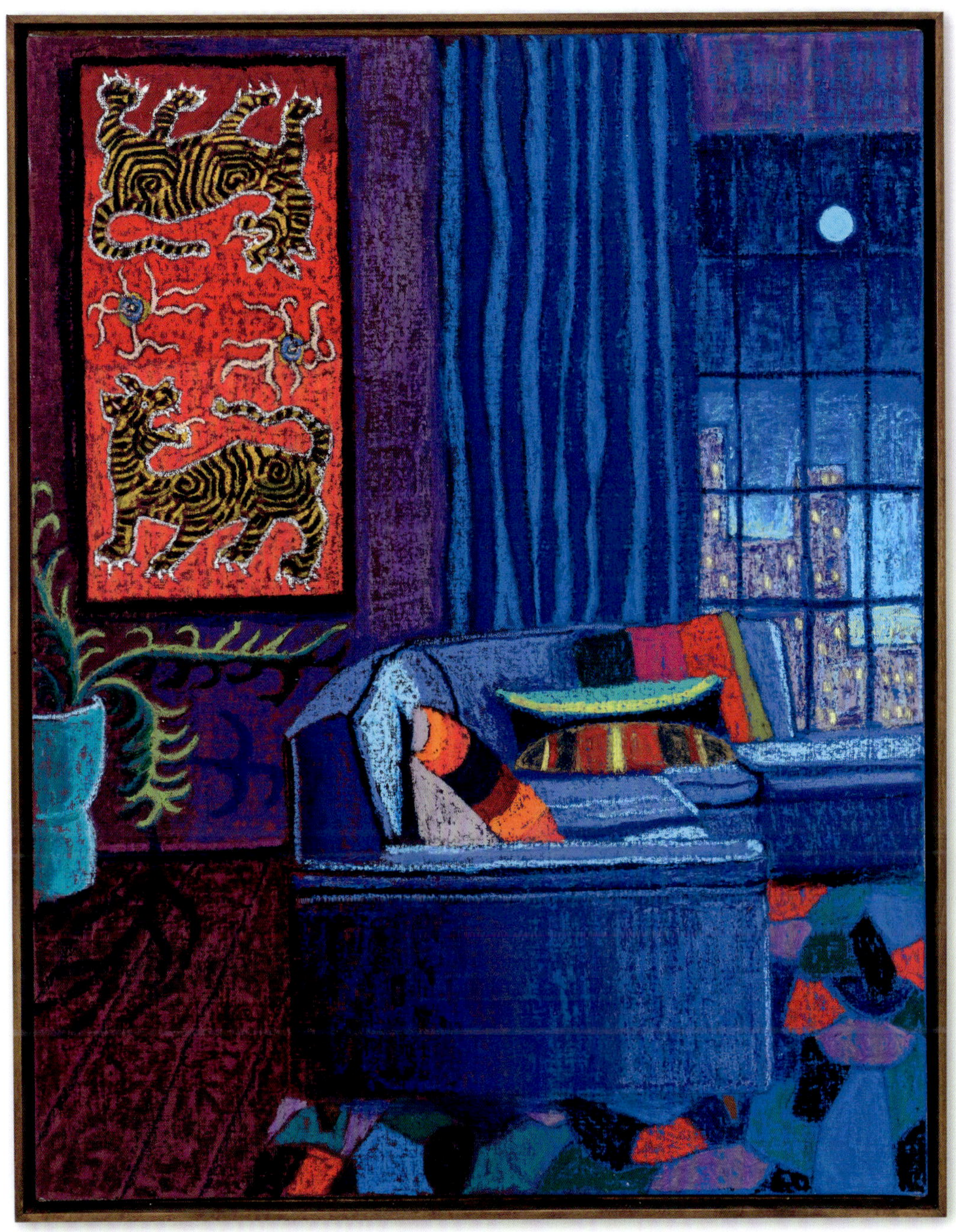

NYC Interior with Tibetan Tapestry, 2021, oil stick, oil pastel, and Flashe on linen, 30 x 24 inches

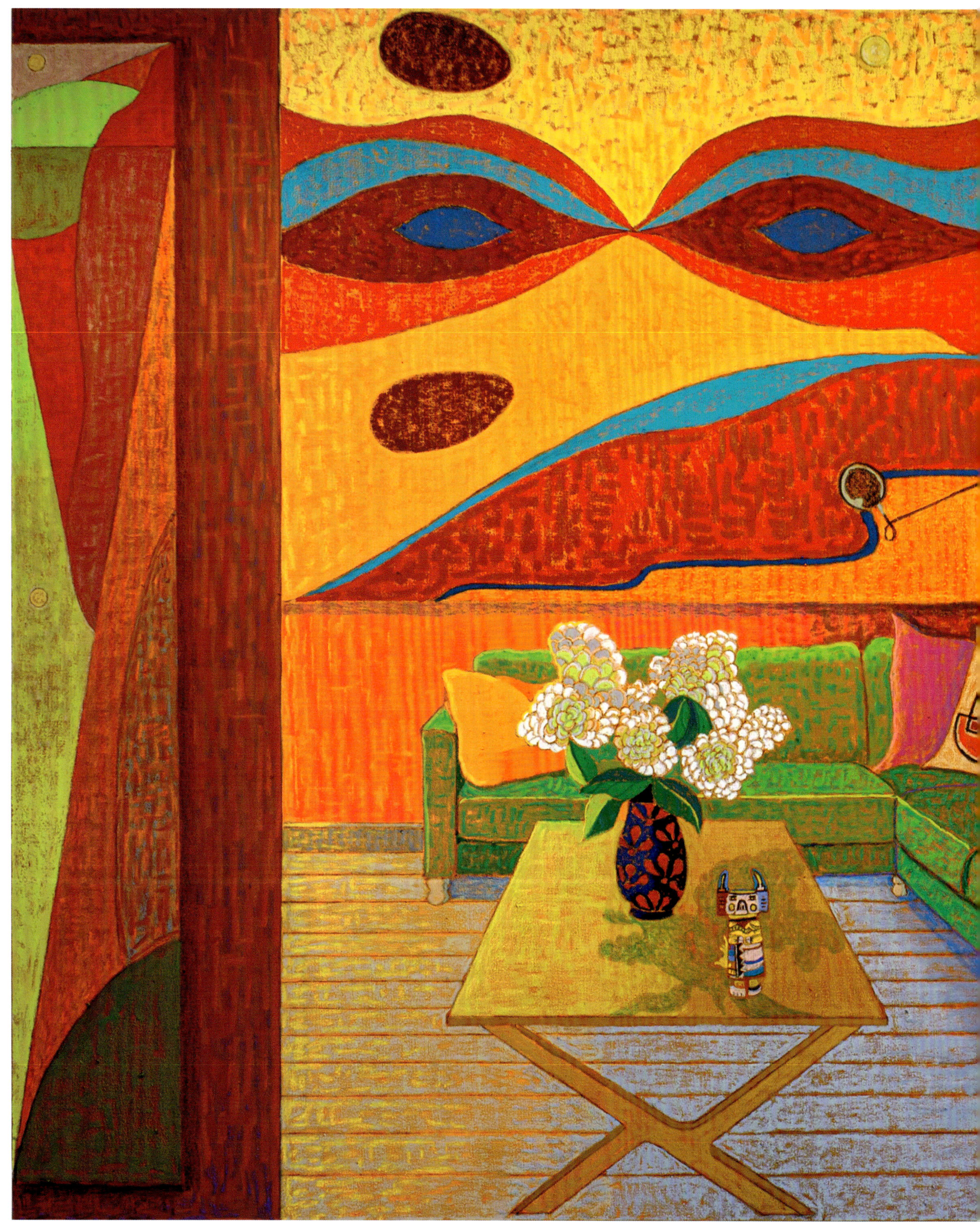

New American Painting, 2021, oil stick, oil pa

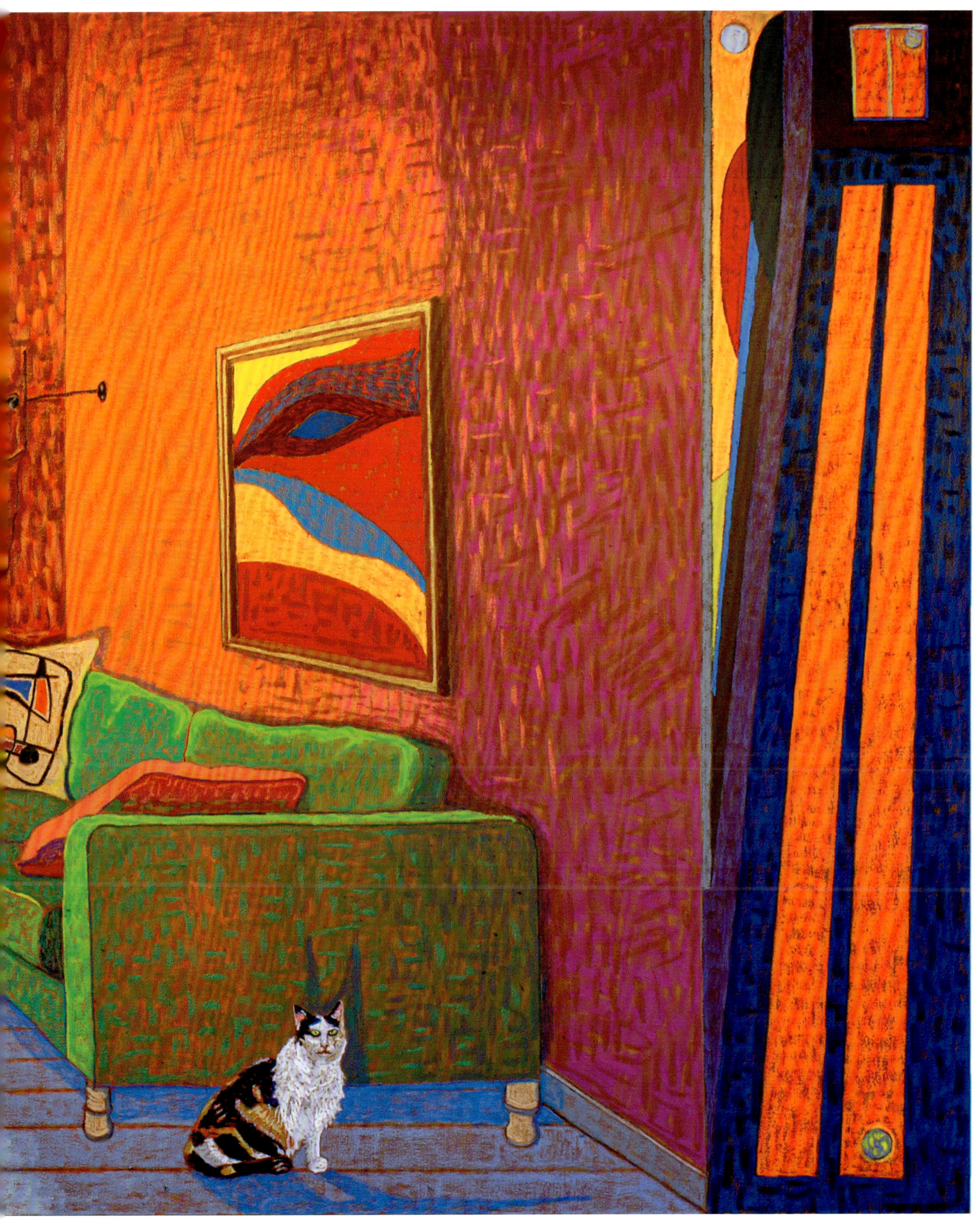

d Flashe on linen, 78 ½ x 133 ½ inches

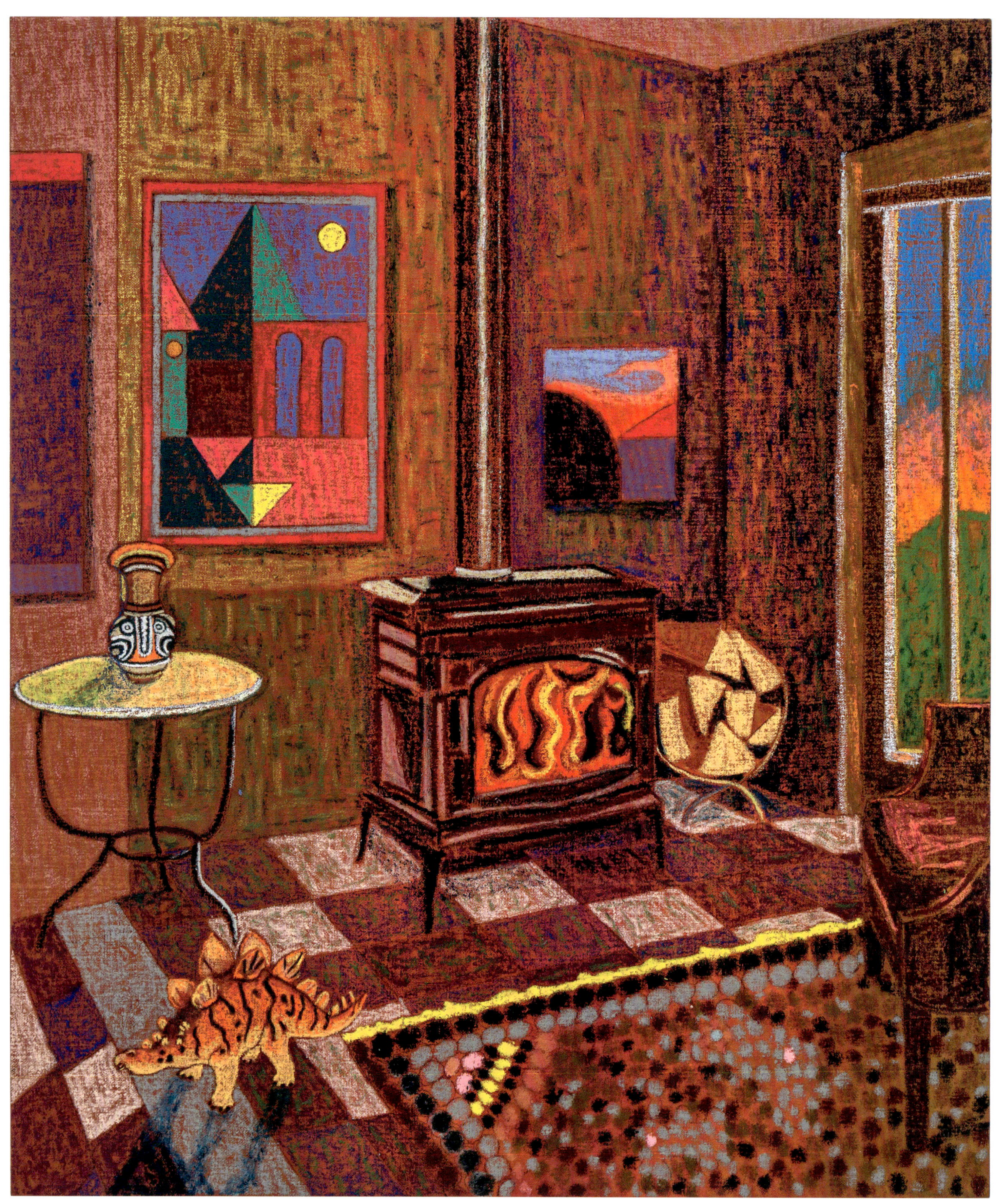

Upstate Interior with Wood Burning Stove, 2021, oil stick, oil pastel, and Flashe on burlap over canvas, 84 x 72 inches

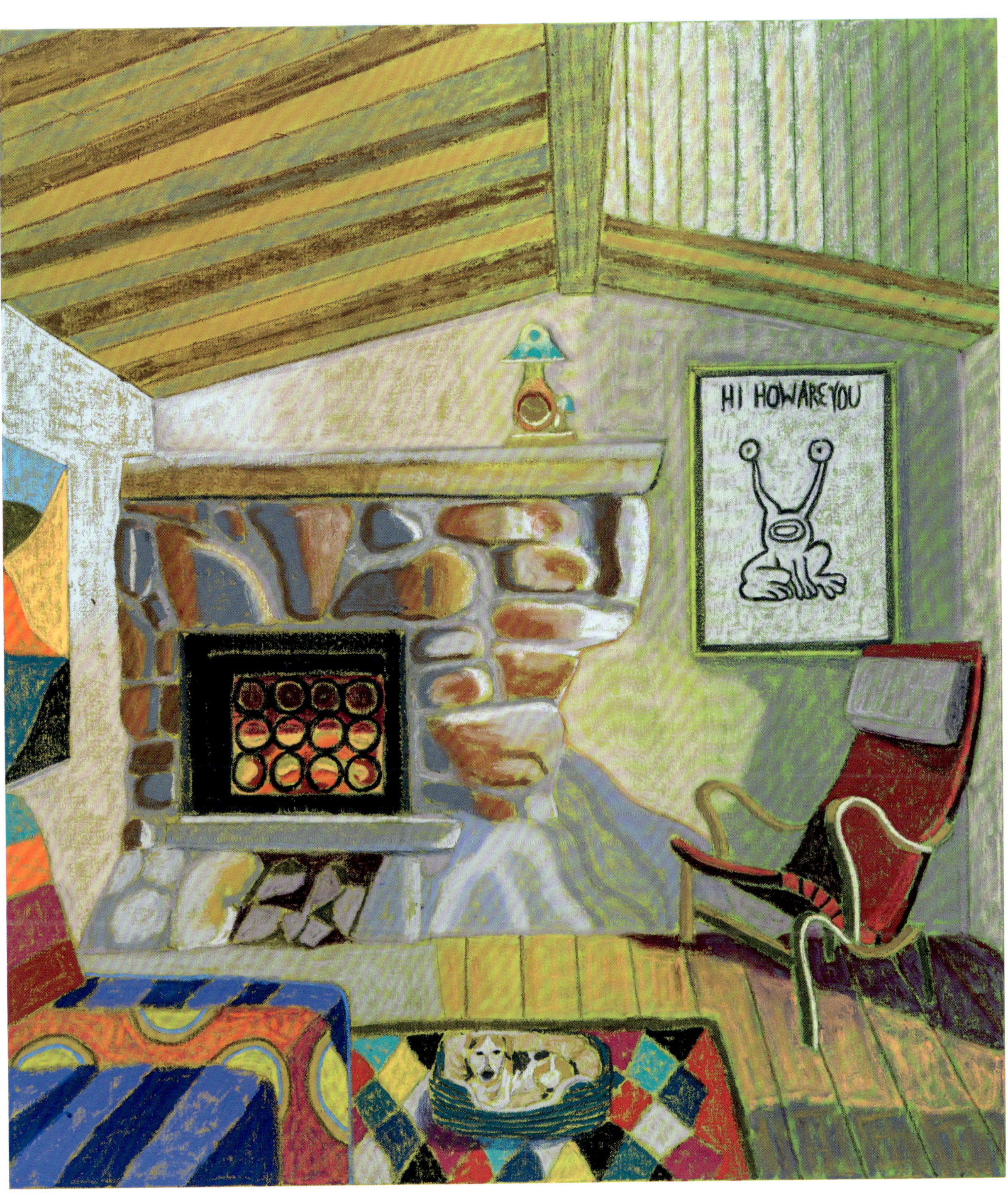

Interior with Daniel Johnston, 2021, oil stick, oil pastel, and Flashe on linen, 46 x 41 inches

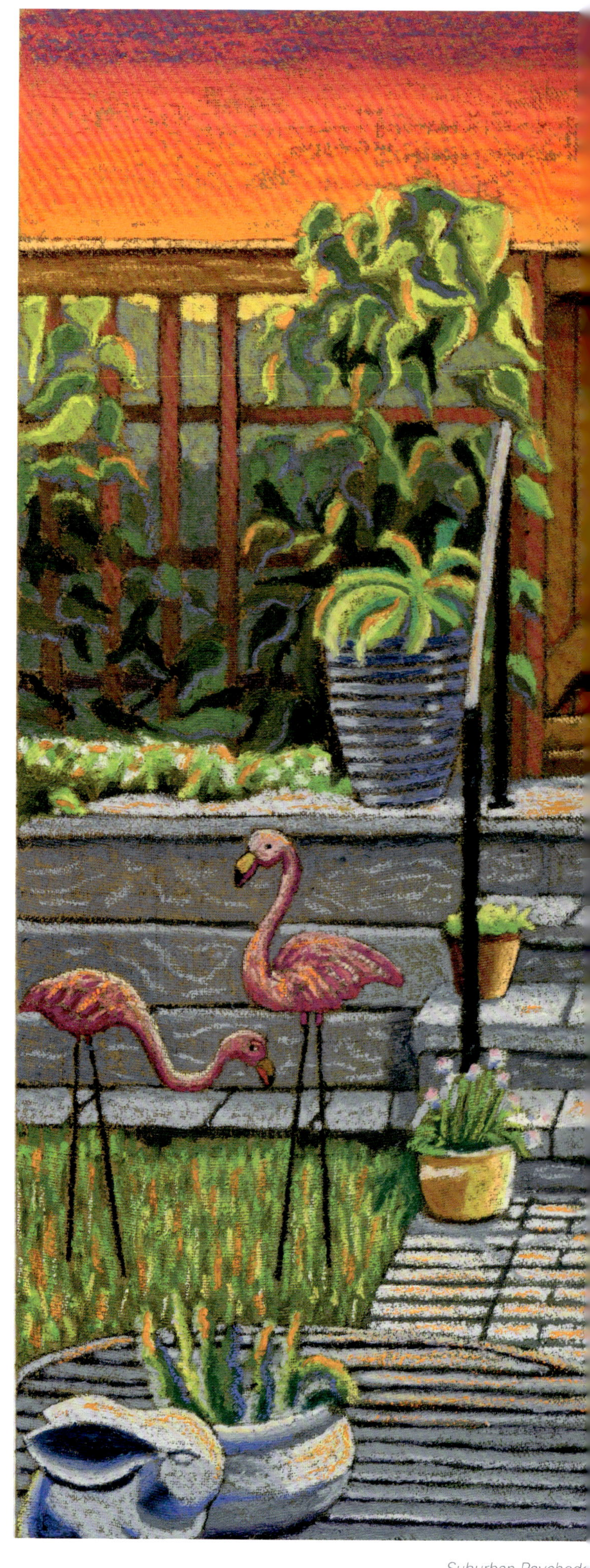

Suburban Psychede

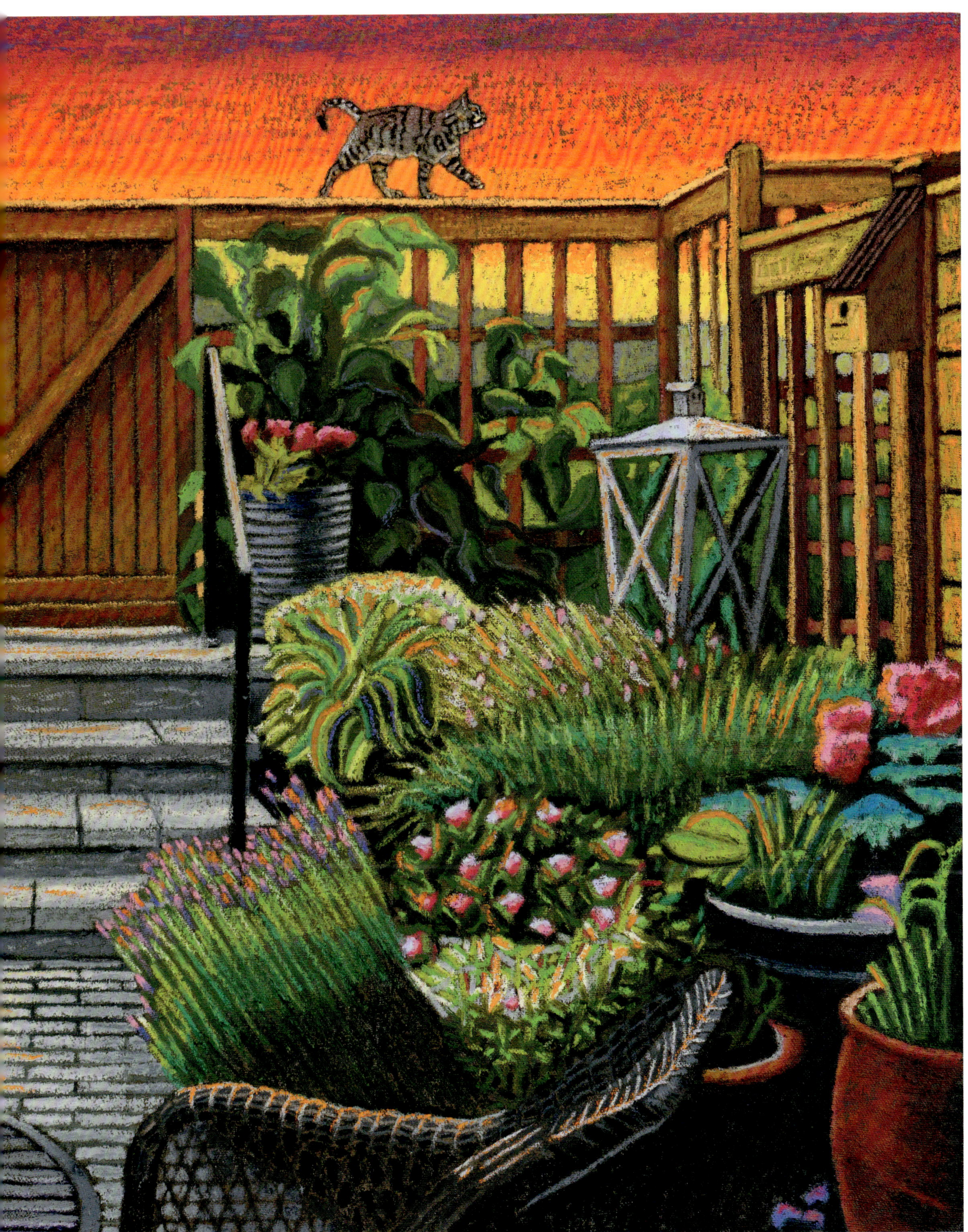

rden with *Plastic Flamingos,* 2023, oil stick, oil pastel, and Flashe on burlap over canvas, 64 x 80 inches

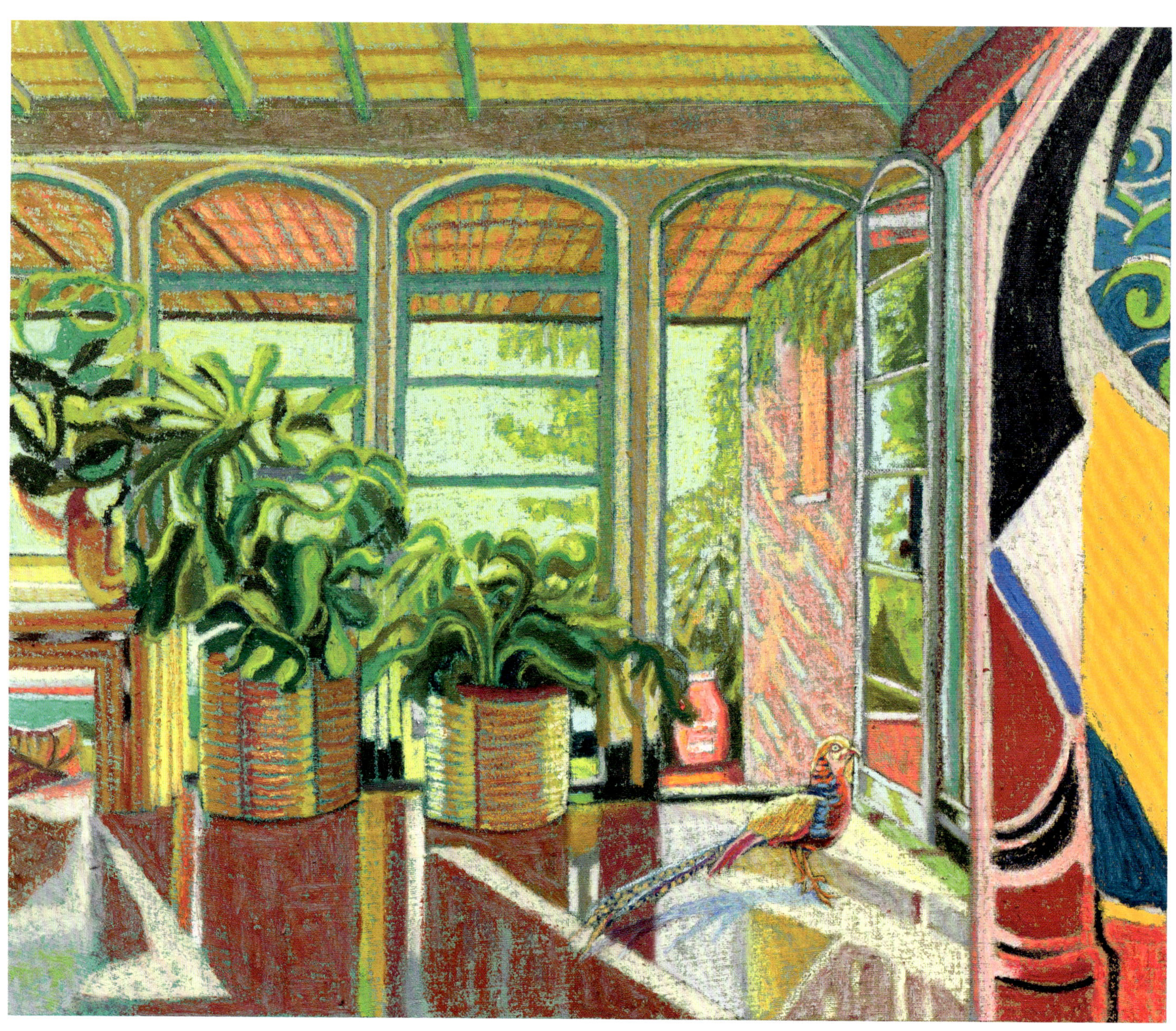

Flamingo Estate with Golden Pheasant & Hockney Screen, 2023, oil stick, oil pastel, and Flashe on burlap over canvas, 50 x 60 inches

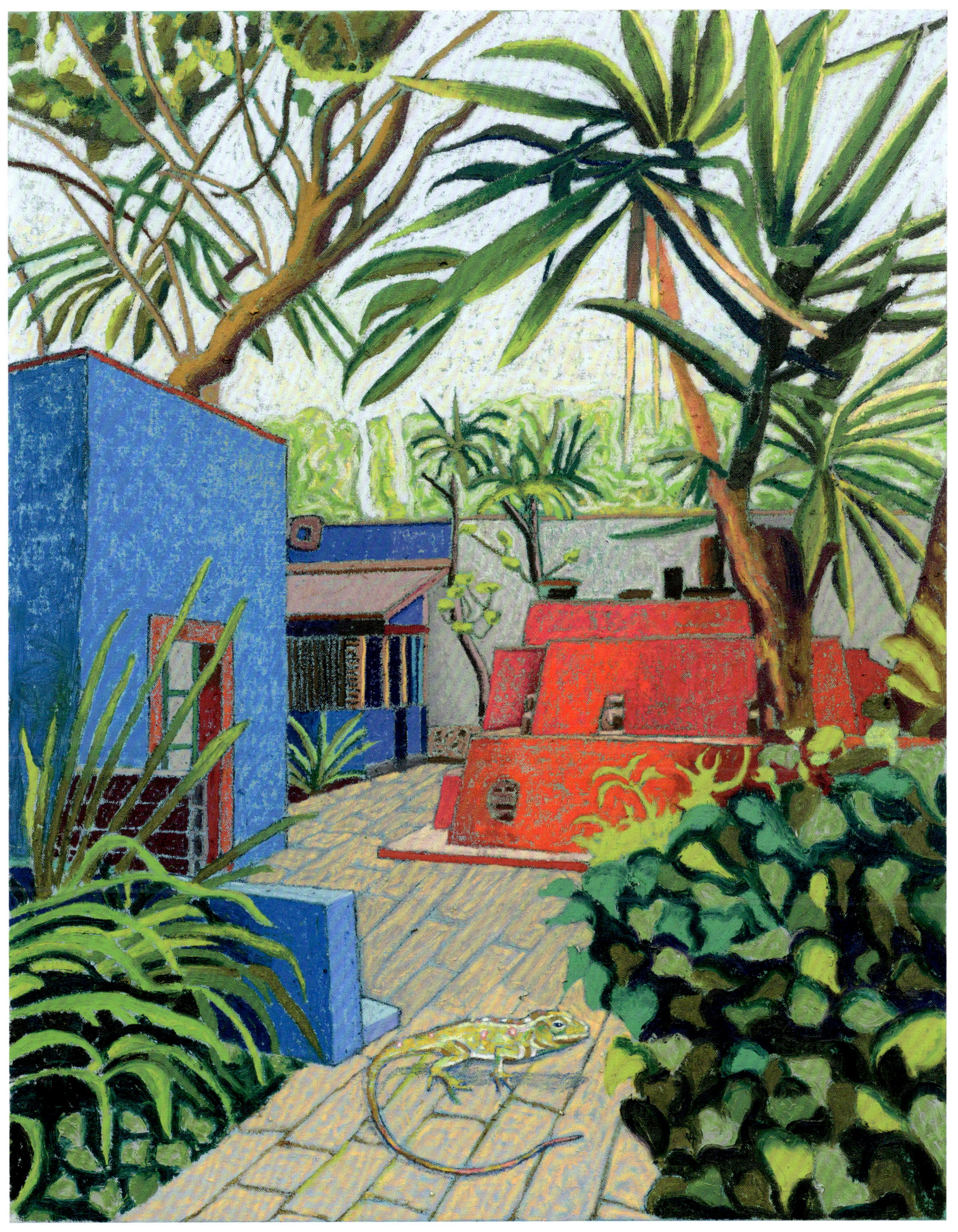

The Garden of Casa Azul, 2023, oil stick, oil pastel, and Flashe on linen, 45 x 36 inches

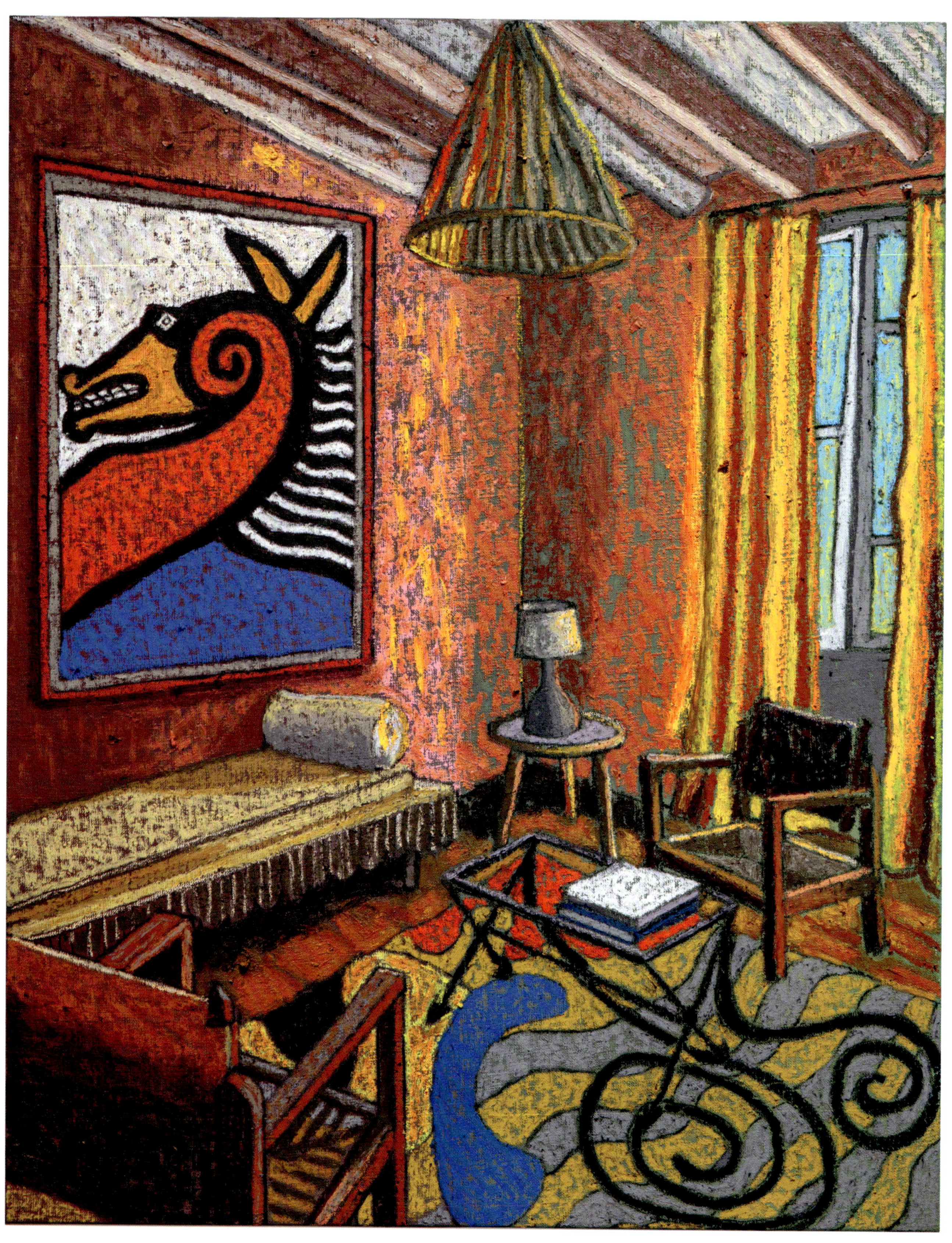

Interior with Calder Lithograph & Calder-Inspired Rug, 2022, oil stick, oil pastel, and Flashe on linen, 30 x 24 inches

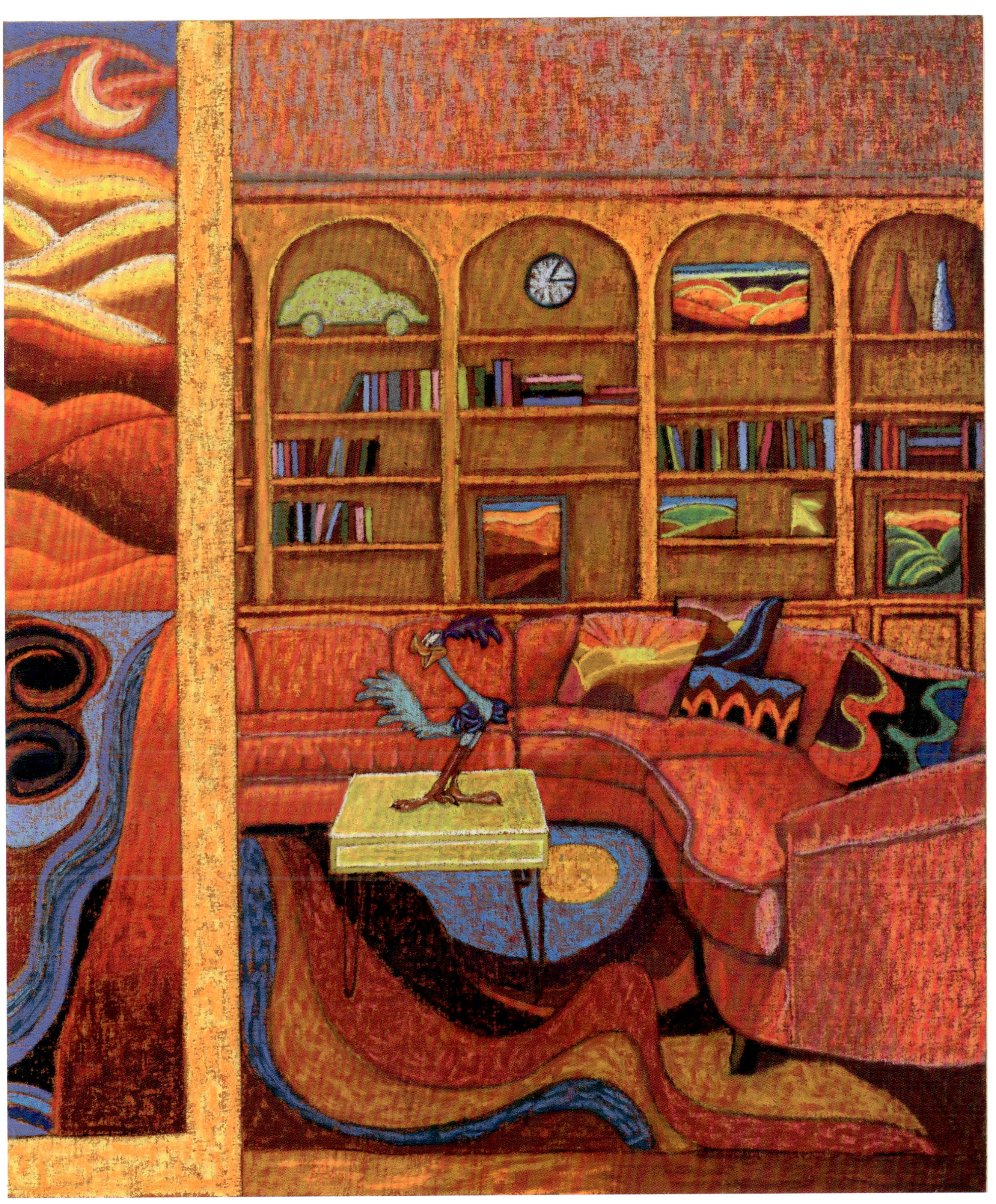

Interior with Road Runner, 2022, oil stick, oil pastel, and Flashe on burlap over canvas, 84 x 72 inches

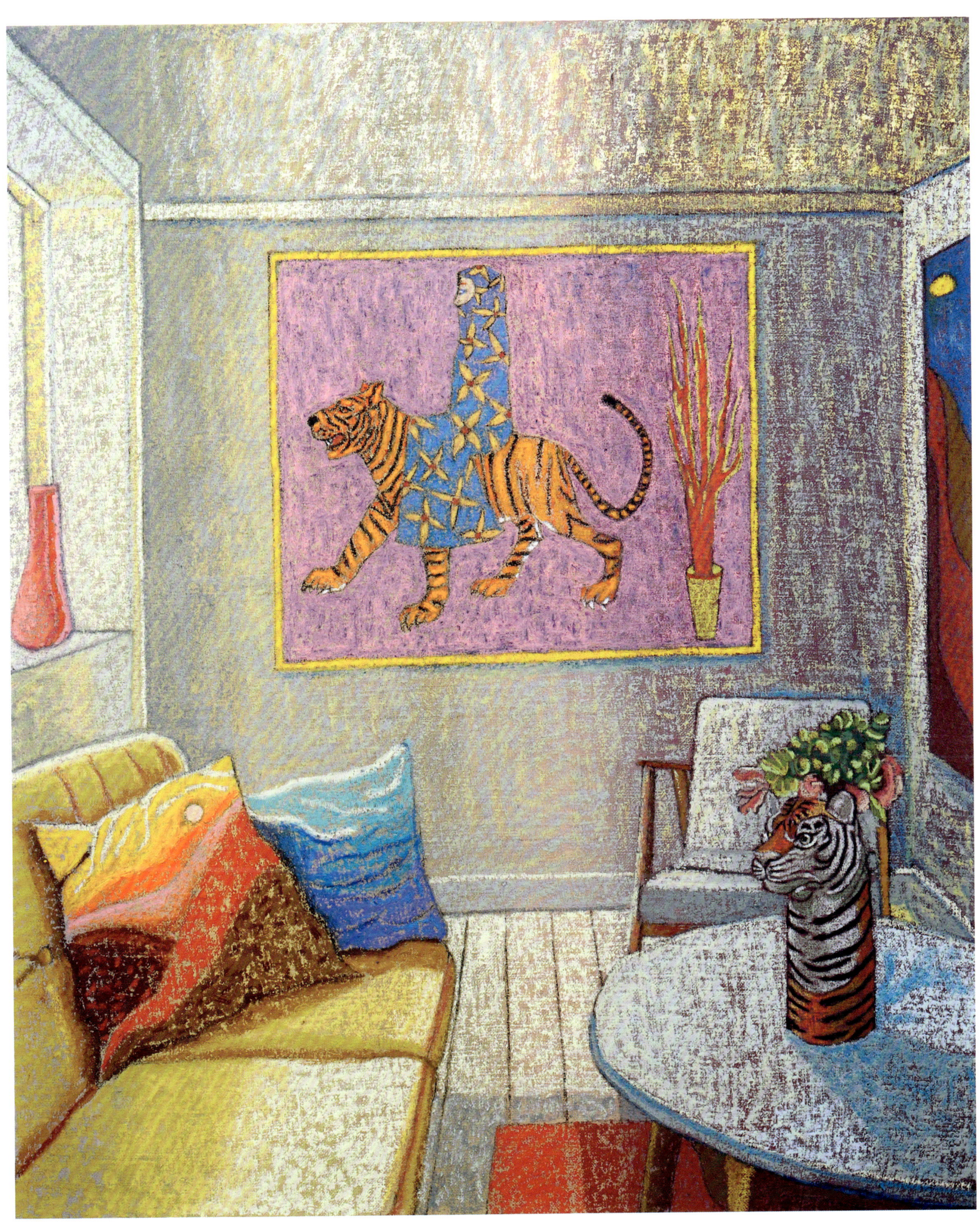

Interior with Joan Brown, 2022, oil stick, oil pastel, and Flashe on burlap over canvas, 72 x 60 inches

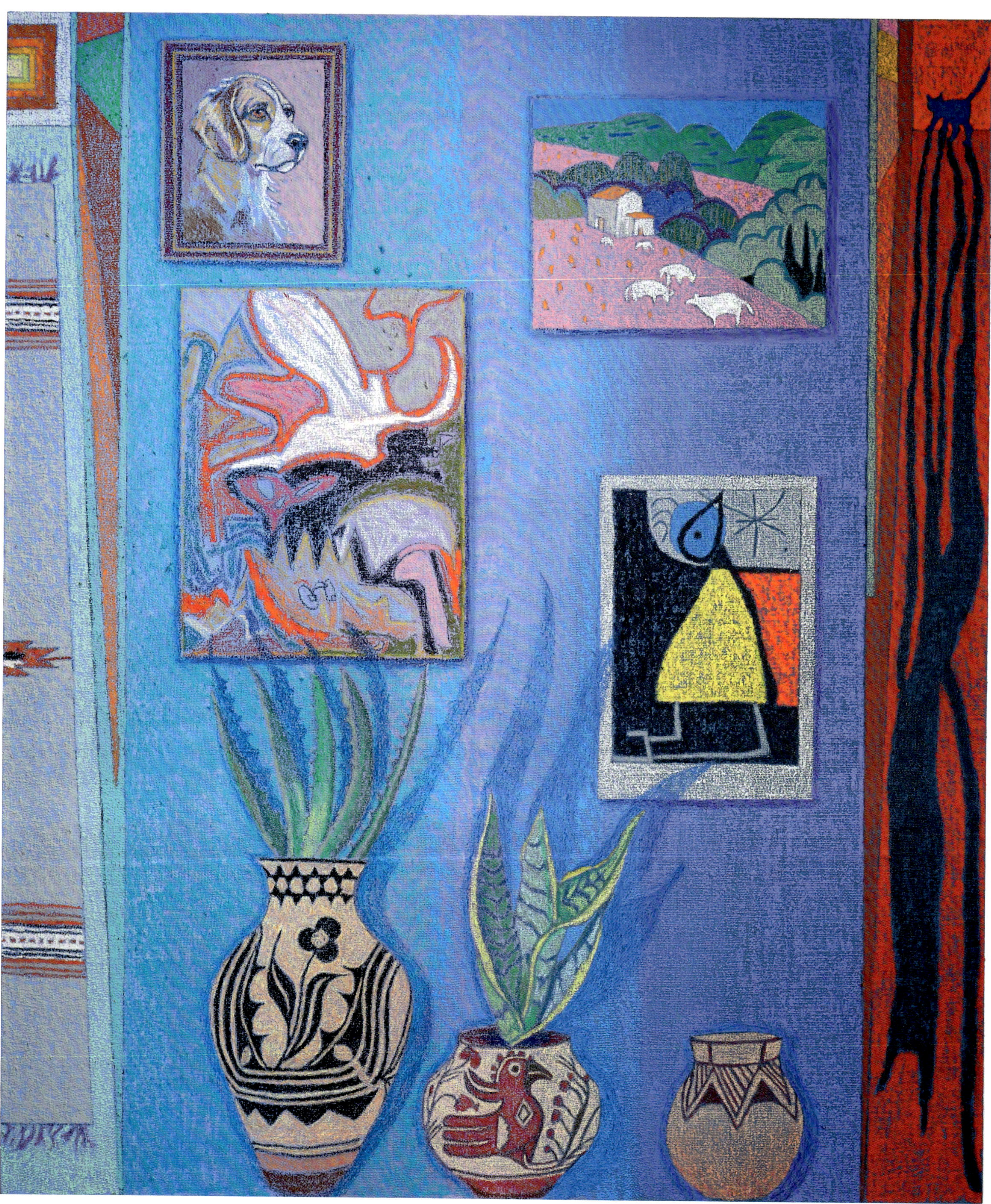

Interior with Thrift Store Dog Portrait (Native American Pottery & Rug, Miró Poster, Colab painting with Jonas & Mary Fedden Painting), 2020,
oil stick, oil pastel, and Flashe on burlap over canvas, 72 x 62 inches

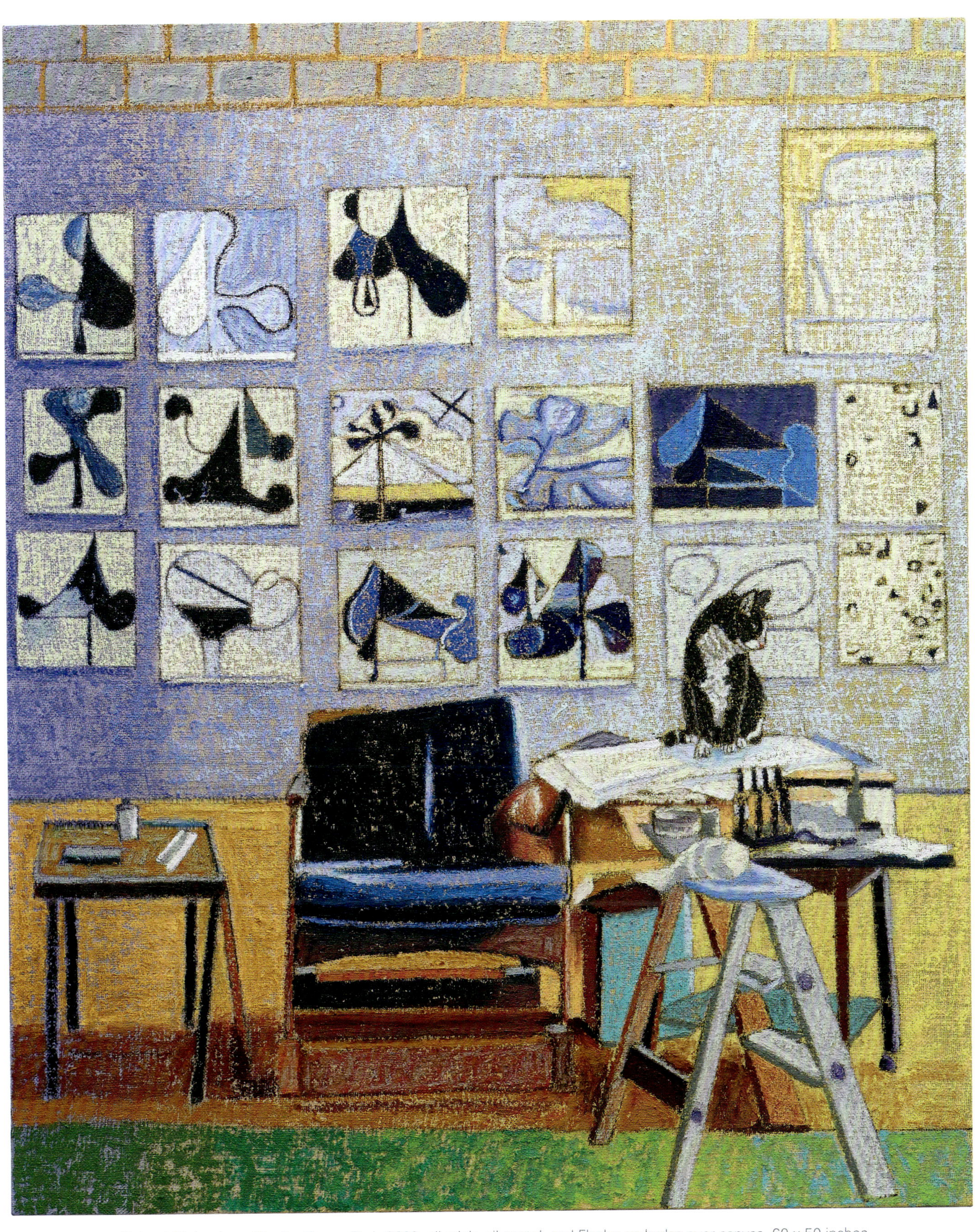

Richard Diebenkorn Studio, Ocean Park, 2023, oil stick, oil pastel, and Flashe on burlap over canvas, 60 x 50 inches

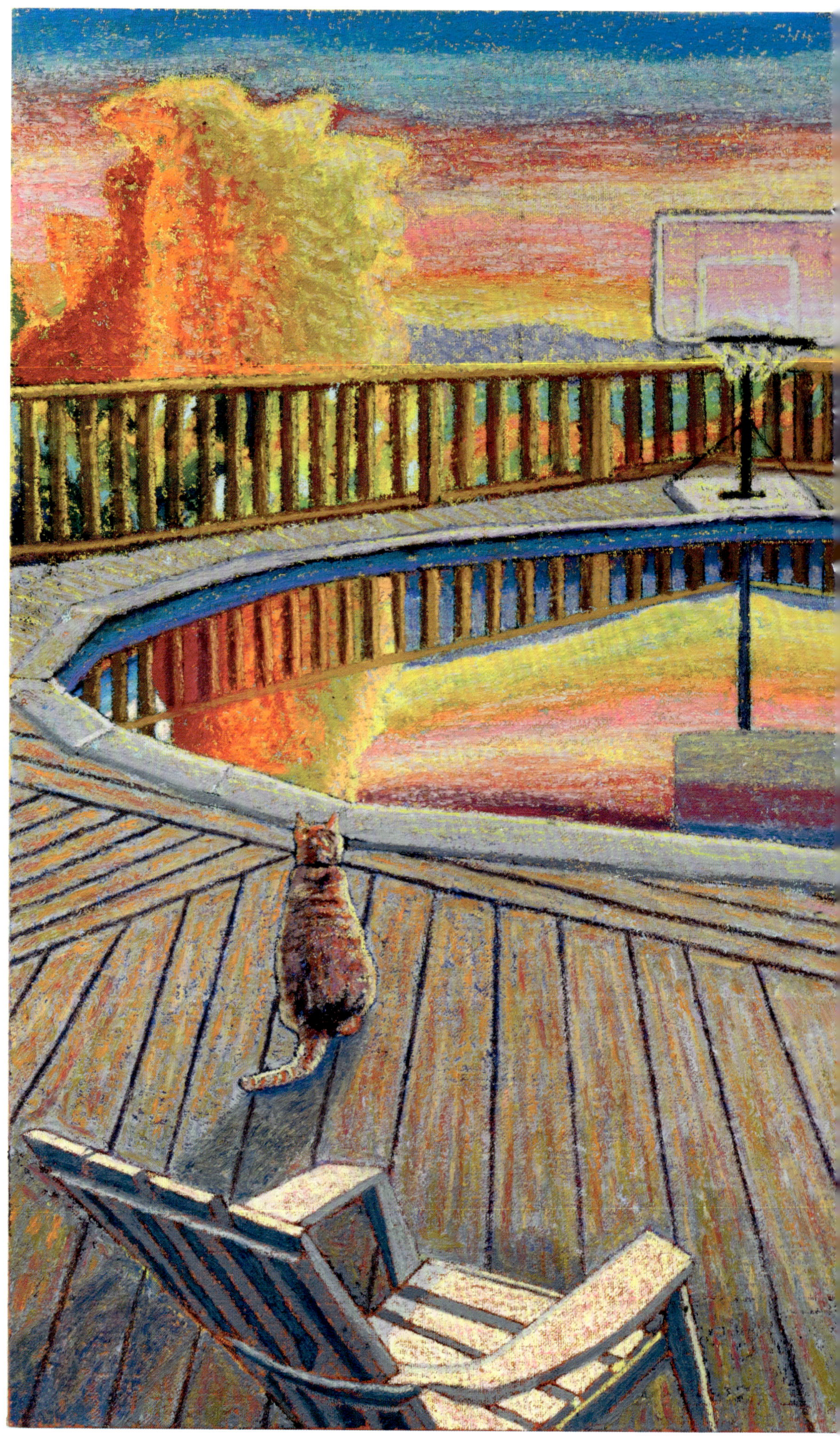

Autumnal Pool Scene, 2023, oil stick, oil paste

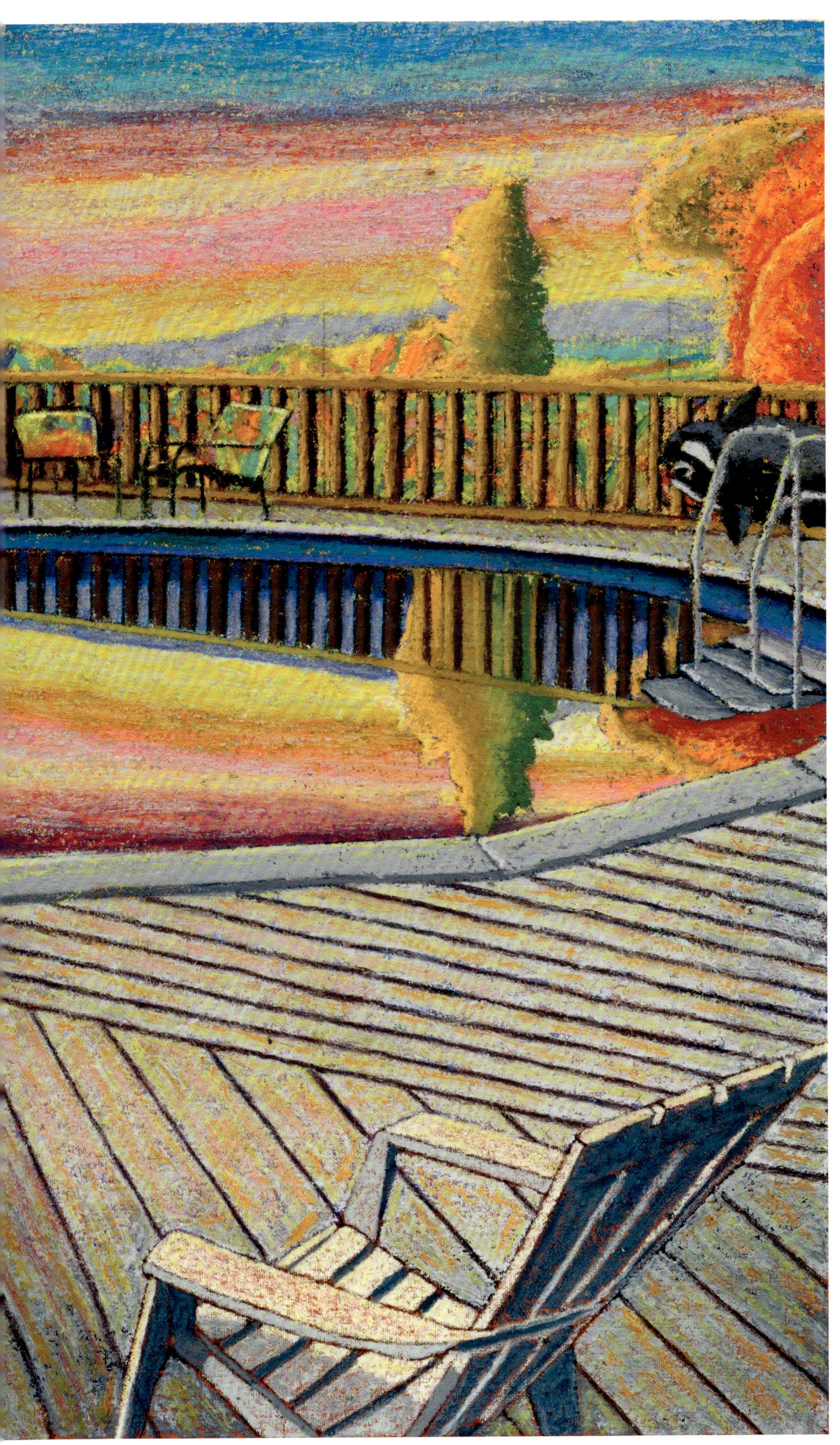

d Flashe on burlap over canvas, 72 x 90 inches

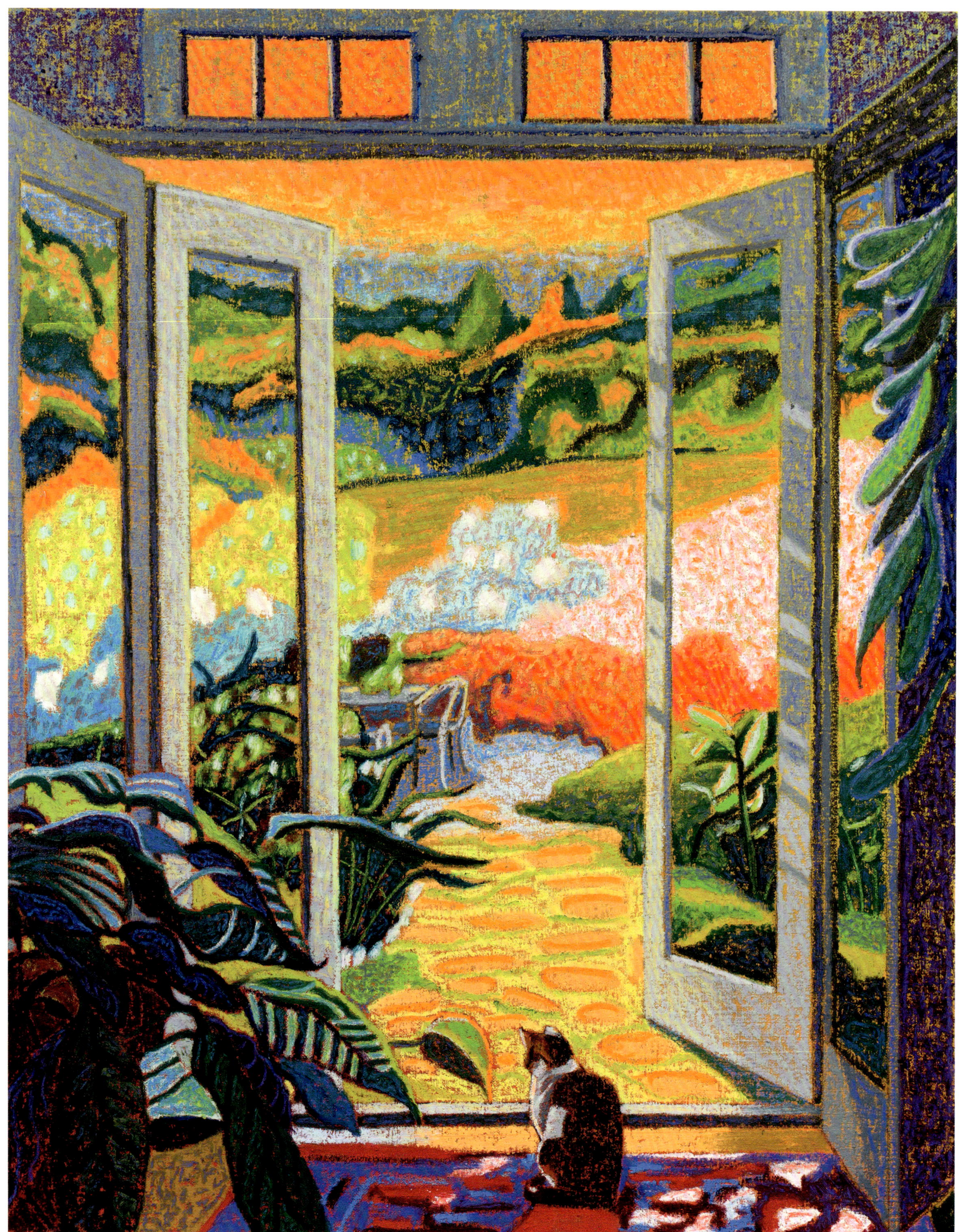

Threshold Painting, 2023, oil stick, oil pastel, and Flashe on burlap over canvas, 85 x 68 inches

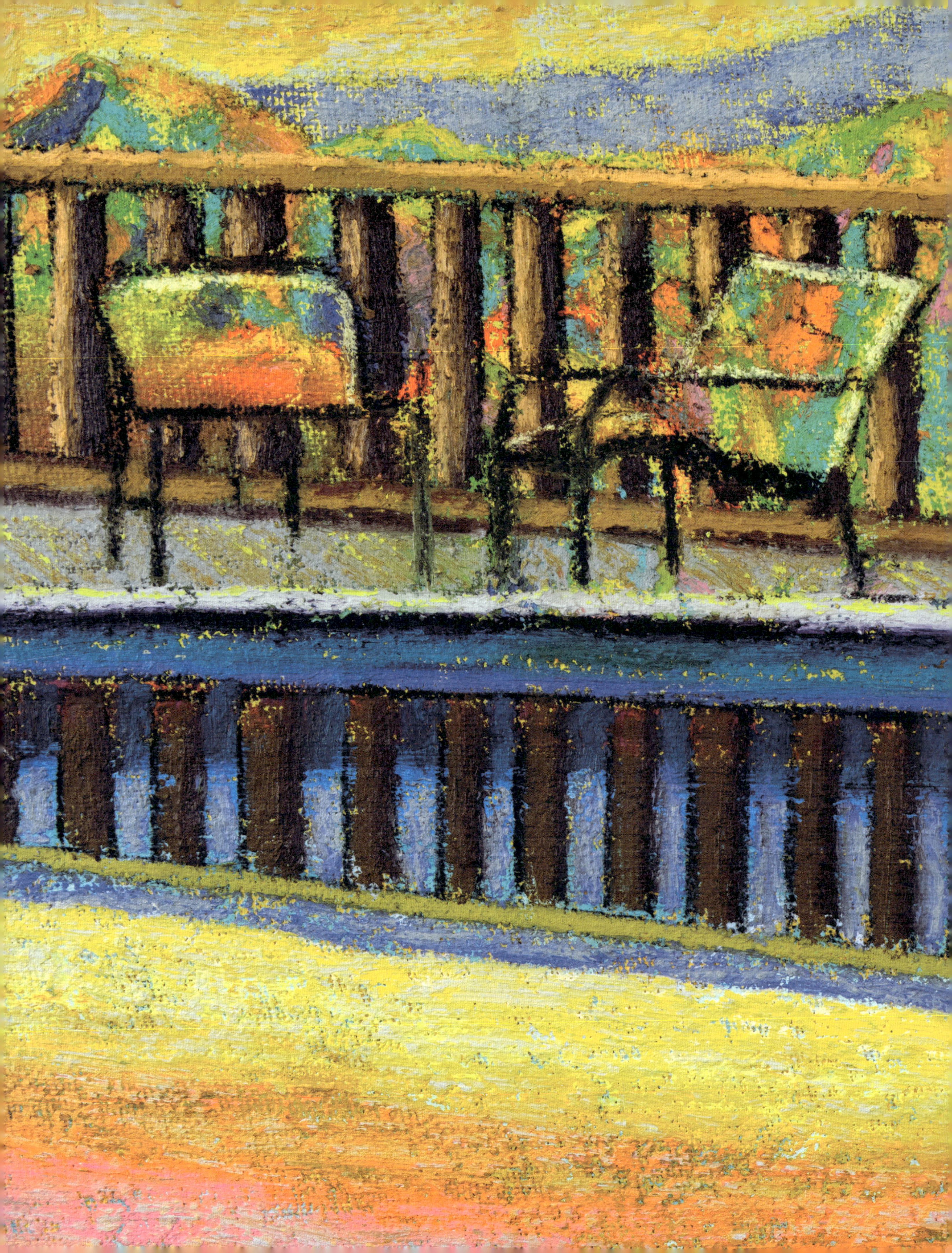